Praise for Reaching for the High Note:

Reaching for the High Note features over 350 artists that contributed to Indiana's music scene. Covering five decades, music historian Larry Goshen's compilations of music history began thirty-two years ago with the publication of *Indy's Heart of Rock 'n' Roll* and 20 years ago with the publication of *Let the Good Times Roll.* Utilizing his expertise as a photographer, music historian, and love of music as a performer, Larry has bettered these books with this one.

Goshen presents fascinating information about the artists who dominated the Indiana music scene during the 1950s, '60s, '70s, '80s, and '90s. Included are sections devoted to jazz and country and western, and a short section on up and coming artists. For easy reading, the artists are listed alphabetically with their brief biographies.

Goshen's contribution is important since he worked tirelessly to preserve historical data regarding the artists. Many of them are instantly recognizable, but Goshen leaves no one out by focusing on those who may have been "one-hit-wonders," or performed for a short time. Regardless of their lack of national fame, they will now never be forgotten.

Reaching for the High Note is important for another reason. While New York City, Los Angeles, Memphis, Nashville, and Chicago are normally given credit as hotbeds of rock 'n' roll, jazz, blues, big band, and country and western, this book provides credibility that Indianapolis and the State of Indiana deserve mention as well.

Good bad or indifferent, Indiana music has for decades held a special place in popular music. *Reaching for the High Note,* features artists from Michael Jackson to John Mellencamp to Hoagy Carmichael to Axl Rose to Wes Montgomery and the Four Freshmen as well as those of lesser renown and is a tribute to the artists that have entertained audiences for more than fifty years! For this we owe a debt of gratitude to Larry Goshen.

Anthony Gourdine
Little Anthony & the Imperials

Reaching for the High Note

AN ANTHOLOGY OF INDIANA MUSIC BY

LARRY GOSHEN

Reaching for the High Note

Published by:

Larry Goshen
1035 Sanders, Studio 121
Indianapolis, Indiana 46203
(317) 264-8126

Goshen, Larry, 1941–
Reaching for the High Note, An Anthology of Indiana Music / Larry Goshen
p. cm.
ISBN: 978-1-955622-82-0 (hardcover)
        978-1-955622-81-3 (paperback)

1. Music 2. Music History 3. Indiana 4. Indiana Music History

First Edition

10 9 8 7 6 5 4 3 2 1

Cover Photograph: Larry Goshen

Dedicated to Larry Goshen's friends:

"Bouncin' Bill Baker,
the inspiration for many young musicians

Delbert Bailey

Paul Hutchinson

Rocky Givans

Acknowledgments

Larry Goshen thanks the many musicians and entertainers who provided their time and effort to contribute to *Reaching for the High Note*.

They include good friend Don Kelley. His many years of friendship and encouragement (and work without pay) helped make this book a reality. Without his helpful push, "I know you can do it attitude!" and generous help, I could not have completed this book. I would like to thank Mark Shaw for his support of the book and his assistance with finalizing the book text. Deniese Summerville for her long laborious work.

I extend special thanks to other encouraging friends and family. They include my daughter Renee, sons Mark and Larry, Jane Varner, Cathy Morris, Mauvene Borton, Monika Herzig, Keith (Keeite) Phillips, Steve Ross, Kyle Long, Leslie Lynnton Fuller, Tilly Gansner, Cindy Goshen and my two brothers Herb and Dale Goshen.

Table of Contents

Author's Note

When I was a kid growing up in the town of Needmore, Indiana, there was no television. But I do remember a radio. My mother would listen to country music. Until age nine, I swallowed a steady diet of Ernest Tubb and Hank Williams.

In 1950, my mother, two brothers and I moved to Indianapolis to be closer to where my father worked. I could finally absorb different styles of music. From age ten until around 13, I was fascinated with Frank Sinatra's "Learnin' The Blues," singer Mindy Carson, and The Four Aces' recording of "Standing On The Corner," the song about watching all the girls go by!

In 1955, rock 'n' roll just stood-up and kicked me in the ass. Chuck Miller's version of "The House Of Blue Lights," started things, and Bill Haley's "Rock Around The Clock," from the movie *Blackboard Jungle* put me in gear. From that moment on, music was my life

While attending Arsenal Technical High School in Indianapolis, I studied flute and French horn before switching to the drums. I focused on drums after I attended a teen dance and heard my first live band. When the band took their intermission, my friends persuaded me to approach the stage and play the drums. I had never played a set before, never even played the drums, but I found the groove. The kids enjoyed the performance. That surprised many people, including the drummer, who was a little uptight.

Excited, I convinced my parents to buy my first set of drums the next day. My dad paid $287 for a Ludwig set purchased at Arthur's Music Store in Fountain Square, Indianapolis. It included a snare and base drum and a 12" Zildjian cymbal. Not much of a set, but it was good enough to learn with. I built it up over the years.

In 1957, my first band was a three-piece group called The Crowns. It included Chuck Ellis (guitar), Danny Beach (guitar), and yours truly on drums. We played Elvis and Carl Perkins tunes. We performed on several television shows, including Jimmy Mack's *Teens 'N Tunes*.

In 1958, I joined pianist Jimmy Ganzberg. We performed as a duo. Jimmy fascinated fans with his impersonation of Jerry Lee Lewis. In 1959, I became a member of Jerry Lee Williams and The Crowns. We recorded one record on the Solid Gold label. The songs were titled

"Wibcee" and "The Go Tune." Both were instrumentals. After member changes, we used the name, Sounds of The Crowns. We continued to perform at record hops and do live stage shows.

In 1959, while performing in Terre Haute, I had the good fortune to appear on stage with singer Jackie De Shannon. Our group handled the sound check for Jackie and we performed on the same show. She was very young, around 16, but her performance was one that I will never forget.

In 1963, I joined the road group, The Five Checks. For two years, we toured the Midwest.

Many special moments have occurred since then. Music has always been a special part of my life. I still perform once in awhile, but my main interest is to capture the past and present, preserving the music, the singers, the musicians and the entertainers that were so enjoyable.

Music truly does make the world go around. It affects our moods and adds to everything we do. Can you imagine a film without music surrounding the scenes — making us laugh, making us sigh or making us cry? Without music, there would be no dancing. Can you imagine that?

The entertainers mentioned in this book deserve an Indiana Musician's Hall of Fame. Until that occurs, I hope this book is a living tribute to their achievements.

— Larry Goshen

Explanation of Categories in This Book

Segregating artists into various categories for this book was extremely difficult. The question may arise: Why is a particular artist included in a certain category? The answer is that selection was based on when the artist or artists were best known. In some instances, a classification was made due to the start of a music career.

When difficulty is encountered finding an artist or artists, check several categories. Future editions will include additional artists.

THE CATEGORIES

The Fantastic Fifties

This section is dedicated to entertainers that performed mostly for teenagers during the birth of Rock 'n' Roll and R&B. Many of the artists performed later in their careers in other ventures.

The Sensational Sixties

This section is based on the artists and music targeted at teens and young adults. Garage bands and musicians that played affected the music of today

Nightclubs, Bars, and Music Stars of The Sixties

This section features musicians and singers that performed in nightclubs and bars in the Indianapolis area and across the nation in the 1960s.

The Swell Seventies

The Emphatic Eighties

The Naughty Nineties

This section includes prominent groups that gradually became professional and popular entertainers. The 1990s includes jazz groups along with pop and rock because some musicians during this era performed in multiple musical categories.

Country & Western Guy and Gals

While not a complete roster of Indiana country performers, this section recognizes artists with roots in Indiana.

Jazzmakers

Indiana jazz performers deserve a book of their own, but this section highlights several that were notable.

The Fantastic Fifties

The Fantastic Fifties

Post-World War II America was a melting pot for change. Dwight D. Eisenhower became President in 1953, Senator Joseph McCarthy launched his drive to rid the country of communists a year later, and blacks boycotted segregated city bus lines in Montgomery, Alabama in 1956. By 1959, New York City authorized their city council to investigate the potential for it to become the nation's fifty-first state.

On the cultural scene, *All About Eve* won the Academy Award in 1950. Grace Kelly was a movie star as was Marlon Brando, who was featured in *A Streetcar Named Desire*. Dr. Seuss wrote *The Cat In The Hat* in 1957. Lillian Hellman penned *Toys in the Attic* three years later.

When the year 1950 dawned, popular songs across America included "If I Knew You Were Comin' I'd Have Baked A Cake," "Mona Lisa." "I've Got The Word On A String" and "The Tender Trap." During this decade, such hits as "Hello Young Lovers," "House of Blue Lights," "The Green Door," "Smoke Gets In Your Eyes," and "Purple People Eater" lit up the charts. Elvis Presley chipped in with "Hound Dog" and "Don't Be Cruel." Bill Haley shouted "Rock Around The Clock" to the delight of his fans.

In Indiana, memorable moments were spent at sock hops and teen dances. The Whiteland Barn was a highlight. Music lovers could stand outside and hear the sounds of a rock drummer beating away. Inside, the stomping feet of the rockers could be felt from the loft above. The Barn was so packed, it's a wonder it didn't topple.

Built in the 1930s, the Barn was originally a square dance hall. Around 1957, owner Don Holt hosted the first teen dance. Seventy-five teens (only three were girls) showed up on a Sunday night. But word spread and the dances became a ritual for every teen that could find their way to Whiteland.

Local disc jockeys "Bouncin' Bill" Baker, Jack Morrow, and Jim Shelton spun the platters. Indiana groups such as the Downbeats, Crowns, and Keetie and the Kats provided live music. In later years, the Barn hosted such international celebrities as Jerry Lee Lewis, Chubby Checker, Duane Eddy, Dee Dee Sharp, Johnny and the Hurricanes, The Kingsmen, The Fireballs, Ray Stevens, Bill Black's Combo, and Conway Twitty, then a rock star. The Barn finally closed in the late 1960s, when rock concerts began to draw teens in droves.

Other popular teen clubs during the late 1950s and early '60s were the Westlake Beach Club and the Indiana Roof. Small community centers such as the First Presbyterian Church (16th and Delaware), Fletcher Place, and Brookside Center were popular venues for music. Groups played anywhere they could find space: shopping centers, swimming pools, and during intermission at drive-in theatres. Many drive-in restaurants featured music and DJs — Merril's Hi-Decker, Al Green's, and Pam's Drive-in to name a few. Rock shows were held at the Speedway Theatre and teens danced at the old Wagon Wheel.

Besides Bill Baker, Jim Shelton and Jack Morrow, disc jockeys included Johnny Spring, Hal Fryar, Bernie Herman, Frank Prater, Tom Mathis, Dick Summer, and Easy Gwynn. Bill Baker, a great entertainer and hilarious comedian, was unique. Many times he dug into his own pocket to pay bands a bit extra. He was also a friend to all — musicians, teens, fans, and everyone.

*T*he teen bands of the 1950s played rock-a-billy, twangy rock, and basic rock n' roll. Those Great sounds should never be forgotten. Many are still classics today. What follows is a tribute to those who played and gained fame, and those who played but did not. Regardless, they all contributed to the enjoyment of music loves during the *Fantastic Fifties.*

Art Adams

ART ADAMS (1960)

Indianapolis-based Art Adams began his music career circa 1959 by playing rhythm guitar and singing with a four-piece country group. This band entertained at picnics, car lots and the country barn in Whiteland. They even performed on local radio shows. Later, in 1959, drums and another guitar were added, and The Rhythm Knights was created. While working teen dances with a local television disc jockey named Jim Laythrop, Art and The Rhythm Knights were give a chance to record. In 1960, Art recorded for the Nashville record company, Cherry Records. He earned attention with his recording of "Rock Crazy Baby." He later played the nightclub circuit and performed at the White Front, Play-mor and other nightspots in the Indianapolis area.

In 2002, after a few years of retirement, Adams' music career was revived due to the popularity of his old recordings overseas. He has since toured Vegas, France, Spain, England, Switzerland, Canada and other points around the world.

In 2021, at age 89, he is recovering from back surgery and plans to continue touring. His recordings include "Rock Crazy Baby"/"She Don't Live Here No More" (1960), and "Dancin' Doll"/"Indian Joe" (1960) on Cherry Records. In 2017, he completed a special recording at the Sun Studio in Memphis, Tennessee titled "Memphis Dream."

Art Adams and The Rhythm Knights

Band members include:

Art Adams
Ky Curley
Ray Gadberry
Harold Knight
Eddie Wiel

Pictured are: Art Adams & The Rhythm Knights (1960) Left to right: Roy Robinet, Ray Gadberry, Eddie Wiel, Harold Knight, Art Adams, front.

"Bouncin' Bill" Baker

Born in Tarentum, Pennsylvania, Bill Baker first experienced the world of entertainment at the age of six by singing live on radio station WWSW. He later played drums with a band called Jive Five. Baker moved to Indiana around 1954 and made his Hoosier radio debut at station WIOU in Kokomo. Around 1956, Baker was hired by station WIBC in Indianapolis as the announcer for the *Burn't Toast and Coffee* program. He became the highest rated DJ in Indianapolis history. In 1962, Baker was named Disc Jockey of the Year by *Mirror Magazine*. Baker, an accomplished drummer, is a member of the Disc Jockey Hall of Fame. In 1964, Baker was master of ceremonies for the first Indiana appearance of The Beatles. Charles William "Bouncin' Bill" Baker passed away at the age of 77 on August 12, 2005.

BILL BAKER AT THE INDIANA STATE FAIR.

Boyd Bennett

Boyd Bennett originally from Nashville, Tennessee, moved to Indianapolis in the late 1950s. He purchased the Thunderbird, a popular local nightclub. Boyd signed with Cincinnati's King Records in the mid-1950s. He recorded two hits, "Seventeen," and "My Boy Flat Top." In 1956, Bennett received national attention with "Blue Suede Shoes," recorded on the King Label. Boyd later signed with Mercury Records, and recorded a lesser hit titled, "Boogie Bear." Boyd Bennett died, June 2, 2002.

BOYD BENNETT (1955)

The Blue Angels

THE BLUE ANGELS

Group members include:

Bud Osborne
Buddy Parish
Richie Schatz
Denie Smerdel

Formed in the summer of 1960, the original group was comprised of Denie Smerdel, Bud Osborne, Richie Schatz and Buddy Parish. Members changed through the years, but Osborne and Smerdel remained as the nucleus. In September 1963, Osborne entered college. Greg Galbraith joined the band for a year before it disbanded. Galbraith later moved to Nashville, where he became a well-known studio musician.

BOYD BENNETT AND BIG MOE

The Boppers

Group members include:

Charles Anderson
Jimmy Anderson
Rudy Bartlett
Jimmy Guilford
Tomas Mitchell
Bill Mosley

THE BOPPERS (1952)
Left to right: Jimmy Anderson, Charles Anderson, Tomas Mitchell, Jimmy Guilford, Rudy Bartlett and Bill Mosley

The Boppers were members of several groups formed in the 1950s, including the Four Sounds and The Monograms. Singer Jimmy Guilford became a member of the famous Lamplighters.

Jimmy Clendening

Indiana-born Jimmy Clendening was a popular singer with teens in the late 1950s. As a featured singer with the popular Keetie & The Kats band, Jimmy recorded "That's The Way," and "Dreamers Romance," a 45 single release on the K-W label.

JIMMY CLENDENING WITH KEETIE & THE KATS
Left to right: Dave Ellman, Larry Lee, Jimmy Clendening, Keith Phillips and Norm Shafey

Jimmy Coe

Although not from Indiana, Indianapolis has been Jimmy Coe's home for more than seventy-five years. He was born in Tompkinsville, Kentucky, March 20, 1921. An established Jazz musician, Coe performed with many great artists, including Freddie Hubbard, J.J. Johnson and Wes Montgomery. In 1953, Jimmy recorded 12 songs for States records. One of the recordings, "After Hours Joint," sold over 300,000 copies. Performing on this recording with Coe were James Palmer (piano/organ), Earl "Fox" Walker (drums/talk) and Remo Biondi (violin/guitar). In 1958, Coe recorded a local R&B hit titled "Wazoo" on the Note label. Collaborators were Henry Cane, Will Scott and Earl "Fox" Walker. Coe's recording of *Cold Jam for Breakfast* (1966) was on the Intro label. His earlier recordings, "I Got It Bad and That Ain't Good" and "Cole Tater" were recorded on King Records under the name of Jimmy Cole. James R. "Jimmy" Coe passed away at the age of 82 on February 26, 2004. (Also see Jimmy Coe in the Jazz section)

JIMMY COE ORCHESTRA

Front (left to right): Ray Smith, Vincent Stewart, Jimmy Coe and Sim Graves. Back row (left to right): Eldridge Morrison, Ted Turner, Ernest Griffin, Hillard Duerson and Earl "Fox" Walker.

The Contemporaries

Band members include:
- **Al Finnell Jr.**
- **Ermon Hubbard Jr.**
- **Al Officer**
- **Gerald "Corky" Ruark**

This band, under the direction of Al Officer, played R&B, pop, and some jazz. Most of their bookings were at college functions and local dance clubs. Two additional members of this group were Rozelle Boyd, a future Indianapolis city councilman, and Freddie Hubbard.

THE CONTEMPORARIES (1954)

Left to right: Al Finnell Jr., Ermon Hubbard Jr., Al Officer and Gerald "Corky" Ruark

The Counts

Group members include:

Chester Brown

James Lee

Robert Penick

Robert Wesley

Robert Young

The Counts were formed circa 1952 while students at Crispus Attucks High School in Indianapolis. They formed a bond of friendship that lasted through the 20th century. Their first recording, "Darling Dear," was released in 1953. It climbed to number 6 on the national R&B charts. The group's original name was The Diamonds, but they were required to change when a national act used a similar name. The Counts other recordings include "Hot Tamales" (1954), "My Dear My Darling" (1954), "Baby, I Want You" (1954), "Let Me Go Lover" (1954), "From This Day On" (1955), "Sally Walker" (1955), "Heartbreaker" (1956), on the Dot label, and "Sweet Names" (1956) on the Note label.

THE COUNTS

Back row (left to right): Robert Wesley, Robert Penick and James Lee. Front row (left to right): Chester Brown and Robert Young

Scatman Crothers

Benjamin Sherman "Scatman" Crothers was born in Terre Haute, Indiana in 1910. He started his musical career as a 15-year old drummer in a speakeasy band in his home town of Terre Haute. He played a variety of instruments, including drums and guitar, on jazz club band circuits in his early days as an entertainer. Among the people for whom he performed was the notorious gangster, Al Capone. Crothers performed on piano and drums in several bands, most notably with bandleader Slim Gaillard. He later became and actor and performed in many movies and television shows. Just a few of the movies he performed in were *Meet Me at the Fair,* (1953) *Hello Dolly* (1969) and *One Flew Over the Cuckoo's Nest* (1975). A heavy smoker most of his life, Crothers was diagnosed with lung cancer in late 1985. He died of pneumonia on November 22, 1986.

The Crowns

Group members include:
 Danny Beach
 Chuck Ellis
 Larry Goshen

The Crowns performed at many teen venues in the Indianapolis area. They appeared on many local radio and television shows in the early 1950s. Around 1959 (after member changes), they recorded under the name of Jerry Lee Williams and The Crowns. Drummer Larry Goshen was the only original member to continue with the Williams group. This photograph of the Crowns was taken in 1958 at the Eastgate Shopping Mall in Indianapolis before it was enclosed. Chuck (Charles) later became Deacon Charles Ellis, and member Danny Beach passed away September 21, 2016.

THE CROWNS (1957)
Left to right: Danny Beach, Chuck Ellis and Larry Goshen

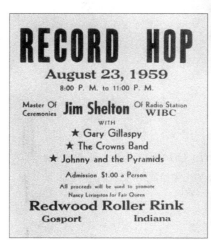

The Dawnbeats

Group members include:

Bob Carrie

Dick Donahue

Don Herald

Phil Ramey

Morgan Schumacher

THE DAWNBEATS (1959)

Left to right: Bob Carrie, Don Herald, Phil Ramey,
Morgan Schumacher and Dick Donahue

The Indiana-based band The Dawnbeats performed in teen clubs such as the Indiana Roof Ballroom. They were a house band that entertained weekends at the popular Whiteland Barn. Featuring guitarist and singer Bob Carrie, the group made one double-sided recording in 1959. The songs were "Drifting" and "Midnight Express" on the AMP label. Morgan Schumacher later performed with rock 'n' roll artists such as Chuck Berry. After the death of Bill Haley, he became the permanent drummer for the touring band, Bill Haley's Comets.

The Deb Tones

Group members include:

Linda Hirt
Karen Lemasters
Julie Wilson

This singing trio was formed in the late 1950s under the name, The Petticoats. They later changed their name to The Deb Tones and recorded for RCA Records. The Deb Tones made many personal appearances in Indianapolis including the Jimmy Mack Television show, *Teen Twirl*.

THE DEB TONES (1958)

The Deb Tones with Jimmy Mack (1958)

Danny Dollar (Dowler)

Danny Dollar was a local singer who possessed a touch of the Elvis sound, and a style and sound of his own. As a teen singer, he excited the girls with his physical actions and artistic voice. Later in his career, he toured the United States and performed with such artists as Bo Diddley and Gregg Allman of the Allman Brothers. In 1967, he recorded *Hello Blues* and *Tell You Like It Is* on the Solid Soul label. Danny Dollar died in August of 2010.

Jackie DeShannon
(Jackie Shannon)

Originally from Hazel, Kentucky, Jackie DeShannon performed many times in the Indiana area. In 1959, she was popular with her version of Elvis Presley's hit recording "Trouble," on the Dot label under the name of Jackie Shannon. She also recorded under the name of Jackie Dee in 1958 for Liberty Records. Her first hit, "Faded Love" also on Liberty Records was released in 1963. In 1964 she was the opening act for The Beatles when they performed their first American tour. In May of 1966, she recorded a Burt Bacharach and Hal David song titled, "What The World Needs Now Is Love." The song was nominated for four Grammies. Many famous artists including Brenda Lee, the Byrds, The Fleetwoods and Kim Carnes have recorded songs that DeShannon wrote.

DANNY (DOWLER) DOLLAR (1957)

JACKIE DE SHANNON

Left to right: Bill Baker, Dale Wright and Jackie DeShannon at a live show in Terre Haute, 1959.

The Downbeats

Group members include:

Bob Carrie
Don Herald
Morgan Schumacher

The forerunner of the popular Dawnbeats band, they re-grouped in 1959 and changed their name to the Dawnbeats.

(See Dawnbeats for information.)

THE DOWNBEATS (1957)
Left to right: Morgan Schumacher, Bob Carrie and Don Herald

*Chuck Berry with drummer Morgan Schumacher
(bass player unknown)*

The Fascinators

Left to right: Larry Fuqua, Lou Corey, Jim Carsey, Boyd "Popcorn" Johnson and Don Kelley. Performing live at intermission for the showing of Elvis Presley's film, King Creole. (Indiana Theatre, Terre Haute, 1958)

Lou Corey, bottom center, (left to right) Larry Fuqua, Jim Carsey and Don Kelley

Don Kelley originally formed the Fascinators in the late 1950s. The Terre Haute group was well known for their great singing and fantastic choreography. The Fascinators performed at the popular Indiana Theatre in Terre Haute. They attracted a large following at the Whiteland Barn, Indiana Roof and Westlake in Indianapolis. Original members included Lou Corey, Larry Fuqua, Boyd "Popcorn" Johnson, Don Kelley, and Jim Carsey. Singer Don Kelley later performed with The Swingin' Lads, a popular Las Vegas act. They appeared several times on the Ed Sullivan and Dean Martin television shows.

Kelley also performed with such artists as Tom Jones, Louis Armstrong, the famous Nicholas Brothers, and many others. In the 1980s and '90s, several successful reunion concerts for the Fascinators were held in Terre Haute. Performing for capacity audiences, each show was as professional and exciting as if it were 1959.

The group's last concert was performed in August, 1997 in Terre Haute with the Terre Haute Symphony Orchestra under the direction of Orcenith Smith.

Front: Jim Carsey, back, left to right, Don Kelley, Don Richetta, Jim Calvin, Larry Fuqua

The Five Stars

Back row, left to right: Larry Huffman, Ron Russell and Bill Campbell. Front row, left to right: Boyd (Popcorn) Johnson and Jimmy Bruhn.

In 1957, music icon Dick Clark said, "'Atom Bomb Baby' is destined to be a national hit." That was the year before one of Indianapolis' hottest singing groups, The Five Stars, appeared on *American Bandstand*. The song recorded on Dot Records reached the number one spot in Indianapolis, but it never achieved the status Clark predicted. Backing up the group on the recording was Boyd Bennett (of "Seventeen" fame) and the legendary saxophonist Jimmy Coe.

The Five stars had debuted circa 1957 when Jim Bruhn joined with four other Indy teens, Bill Campbell, Larry Huffman, Ron Russell and Bruce Miller. Boyd "Popcorn" Johnson later replaced Miller. Their first recording was released on Kernel Records and was later re-released on the national Dot label. Their second recording "Pickin' On The Wrong Chicken," was released in 1958. It earned them a guest appearance on Dick Clark's *American Bandstand*. On this recording, The Five Stars were backed by members of the Count Basie Band. Recordings of The Five Stars include "Atom Bomb Baby"/"You Sweet Little Thing" (1957) Kernel/Dot labels, "Pickin' On The Wrong Chicken"/"Dreaming" (1958) Note/Hunt labels, "My Paradise"/"Friction" (1958) and "Gambling Man"/"Am I Wasting My Time" (1958) on the Note label.

THE FIVE STARS (ORIGINAL GROUP)

Back row, left to right: Ron Russell, Bill Campbell and Larry Huffman. Front row: Jimmy Bruhn and Bruce Miller

The Four Freshmen

Original group members included:

Don Barbour

Ross Barbour

Bob Flanigan

Hal Kratzch

Replacements included:

Ken Errair (1953)

Ken Albers (1956)

Bill Comstock (1960)

Ray Brown (1973)

While attending Indianapolis-based Butler University in 1947, Don and Ross Barbour formed The Toppers. The group included their cousin Bob Flanigan and good friend Hal Kratzch. Since the Barbours, from Greencastle, and Kratzch, a native of Columbus, were freshmen at Butler, they changed the name of the group to The Four Freshmen.

While playing at a nightclub in Dayton, Ohio, the singers were discovered by bandleader Stan Kenton. He arranged a recording contract with Capital Records. The Four Freshmen's recording of "It's A Blue World" became a national hit in 1952. Later recordings such as "Day By Day," "Candy" and "Graduation Day" were successful in the 1950s. In all, The Freshmen recorded more than 30 albums.

THE FOUR FRESHMEN (1959)

The Four Sounds

THE FOUR SOUNDS (1959)
Left to right: Bill Harris, Jimmy Scruggs, Jimmy Guilford and Kenny Moore

Group members include:
Jimmy Guilford
Bill Harris
Kenny Moore
Jimmy Scruggs

The Indiana-based Four Sounds appeared on many top R&B labels, but they never received the recognition they deserved. The Four Sounds recorded for Universal Records, a Detroit-based label, around 1959. They also recorded on the Tuff label around the same time.

In 1961, they released their biggest hit, "Someone To Show Me The Way" on the famous Federal label. Later in the 1960s, Jimmy Guilford teamed up with singer Jimmy Scruggs and became a popular nightclub act in the Indianapolis area.

The Four Sounds' recordings include, "Funny Feeling"/"The Ring" (1959) on Universal Records, a re-release of "The Ring"/"Peters Gun" (1959) on Tuff Records, and "Someone to Show Me The Way" (1961) on Federal.

The Galaxies

Group members include:

Ron Jackson
Larry Parish
Bill Wedsner

Jimmy Ganzberg

Indianapolis-born Jimmy Ganzberg was a graduate of Arsenal Technical High School in Indianapolis. Jimmy played piano at the age of three. During high school, he performed with his own band and made several recordings. Ganzberg attended Indiana University's Jordan Conservatory of Music, studying under jazz icon David Baker. His Jerry Lee Lewis style was very popular. On one occasion, he performed on an open-top piano. To the shock of the audience, the piano's hammers flew out over his head. Ganzberg was a great pianist and entertainer and performed with fantastic showmanship. He later worked his way into soul and jazz, and performed with musicians Marden Baker, Glen Douglas and other jazz artists. His recordings include "Hang Out"/"JoEllen" (1958), "White Saddle Shoes" (1958) and "Rebel Yell"/"Twilight and Tears" (1958), with the Crowns band featuring saxophonist Jimmy Coe. All were recorded for the Indianapolis record label Jet. Ganzberg later moved to Alabama and became a member of the popular Alabama Blues Brothers.

JIMMY GANZBERG (1957)

Left to right: Edgar Bateman, William Boyd, Jimmy Coe, Jerry Lee Williams and Jimmy Ganzberg (Recording session for Jimmy Ganzberg's, "White Saddle Shoes.")

Jimmy Ganzberg with Jimmy Mack and drummer Larry Goshen. (1957)

Larry "Wazoo" Gardner

Versatile bassist Larry "Wazoo" Gardner played with many groups including the popular Keetie & The Kats. Larry toured for a short time with The Five Checks and returned to Indianapolis to perform with the Downbeats and Teach & The Tracers. Larry retired from music and moved to Hiltons, Virginia.

LARRY "WAZOO" GARDNER (1959)

Gary Gillespie

Indiana's Gary Gillespie was one of the first Indianapolis teen idols. He was popular in the late 1950s. Gary performed in local teen clubs and enjoyed top billing in most DJ record shows. He appeared with WIBC disc jockeys Jim Shelton, Bill Baker and Jack Morrow. His first recording, "Honest I Do"/"Dancing Girl" (1961), was released on Delta Records. Gillespie later joined the nightclub circuit singing with groups such as The Katalinas and the By Chantz Operation. His last recording was on BCO Records label. The songs were "Blue Lover," and "My Sweet Cindy."

GARY GILLESPIE (1958)

Hampton Sisters

The Hampton Sisters, Aletra, Carmalita, Dawn and Virtue represent an historical music family. Born in Middletown, Ohio, they learned to play musical instruments when they were three years old. They traveled the country performing with their parents, Laura and Clarke (Duke) Hampton. While playing in Indianapolis in the late 1930s, the family decided to make Indiana their home. Following World War II, the Hampton Sisters played and performed with the family swing group, the Duke Hampton Band. It included family members Clark Jr. "Duke", Maceo, Marcus, Russell and Slide Hampton. The band played through the 1950s & '60s and included such musicians as Dick Dickerson, Gene Fowlkes, Pookie Johnson, Sonny Johnson, Sonny Miller, Bill Penick and Tom Whitted. They performed at the Indianapolis nightclub Steins on North Meridian Street. Later it became Nick & Jerry's. The Hampton Sisters performed with such artists as Nat King Cole and

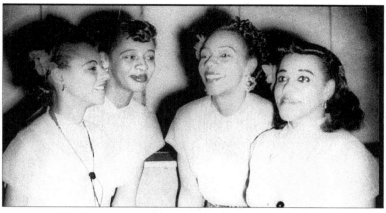

THE HAMPTON SISTERS
Left to right: Dawn, Virtue, Aletra and Carmalita

DUKE HAMPTON BAND
Front row, left to right: Russell Hampton, Carmalita Hampton, Dawn Hampton, Duke Hampton and Thelma Ruth (singer). Second row, left to right: Slide Hampton, Maceo Hampton and Marcus Hampton. Back row, left to right: Virtue Hampton, Aletra Hampton and Sonny Johnson.

Lionel Hampton and played in such historical venues as Carnegie Hall and the Apollo Theatre in Harlem. In 1953, the Hampton Sisters recorded at the King Records studio in Cincinnati. The tunes were recorded with the Duke Hampton Orchestra. They made several recordings, but only one, "The Push"/"Please Be Good To Me" on King records was released. Accompanying musicians on the recording included Billy Brooks, Leo Cornett, Russell Hampton, Iid Ferguson, Slide Hampton, Harry Bell, Thomas Badger, Aletra Hampton, Carmalita Hampton, Marcus "Lucky" Hampton, Virtue Whitted, Dawn Hampton, Calvin Shields and Duke Hampton. Aletra and Virture recorded their first CD on May 21, 2001 with saxophonist Pookie Johnson and drummer Lawrence Clark. Clark "Duke" Hampton died in 2004, and Virtue and Aletra Hampton both passed away in 2007.

Ronnie Haig
(Ron Hege)

RONNIE HAIG

A graduate of Arsenal Technical High School in Indianapolis, Ronnie Haig was born March 3, 1939. ABC-Paramount recordings of "Don't You Hear Me Calling Baby" and "Traveler of Love" (1958) earned Indianapolis native Ronnie Haig an appearance on Dick Clark's *American Bandstand.* Ronnie toured with Dick Clark's Caravan of Stars. He performed guitar on many national recordings, including The Five Stars' recording of "Atom Bomb Baby" (1957). He later recorded on the Note label such tunes as "Rocking With the Rhythm And Blues," and "Money Is The Thing Of The Past." In 1996, he recorded his first CD, *Branching Out,* on the Solid Gold label. Haig was Inducted into Pittsburgh's Roots of Rock & Roll in 1994, and in 1998 became a member of the "Rock-A-Billy Hall of Fame."

Thurston Harris

Indianapolis artist Thurston Harris first gained fame when he sang with the Lamplighters and The Sharps. After this group released twelve singles, Thurston moved back to Indianapolis to continue his solo recording career. In September 1957, Harris recorded a song that Robert Byrd had written titled "Little Bitty Pretty One." It became a top 10 hit. Other Harris recordings included "Do What You Did," and "Over and Over," for Aladdin Records. In 1962 and '63, he recorded on the Cub and Dot Records, and in 1964 moved to the Imperial and Reprise Label. Thurston Harris died of a heart attack in 1990.

Bobby Helms

While performing on his father's local television show, *Monroe County Jamboree*, Bobby Helms was discovered by famed country and western singer Ernest Tubb. This led to an appearance on Tubb's *Midnight Jamboree* and the signing of a national recording contract. Helms gained music immortality with "Jingle Bell Rock," one of the best-selling singles of all time during the Christmas season. He also recorded "My Special Angel," and "Fraulein." Even though Helms was considered a country singer, his songs, recorded for Decca Records, slipped into the pop and rock 'n' roll charts. Helms died in 1997.

BOBBY HELMS (1958)

Chuck Higgins

Chuck (Charles) Higgins was born on April 17, 1924 in Gary. The son of a preacher that played trombone, Chuck, age ten, loved the trumpet. After leaving Indiana around 1940, Chuck settled in Los Angeles, where he played trumpet in his high school band. Years later, Higgins formed his own band and played the saxophone. In 1953, his biggest hit "Pachuko Hop" was recorded on the Combo label. That permitted Higgins to secure concert bookings with Charlie Parker, Nat "King" Cole, Johnny Ace and other big name artists. Albums recorded by Higgins included *Rock n' Roll Versus Rhythm And Blues* in 1959, and *Motor Head Chuck* in 1979.

Joe Hinton

Born on November 15, 1929 in Evansville, Hinton began his musical career in gospel music. Around the mid-1950s, he moved to Memphis where he recorded with the gospel group, Spirit of Memphis. While working for Peacock Records, he switched to R&B music. Joe then recorded "Ladder of Love" (1958), and "You Know It Ain't Right" (1963) for Back Beat Records. The latter climbed to #20 on the hit charts. In 1964, Hinton's soulful version of the Willie Nelson song, "Funny" reached the #13 spot in the top 100. Hinton continued to record for Back Beat Records before dying of cancer in 1968.

Impalas

Group members include:

Bill Lundwall
Jim Padgett
Bill Pierce
Tom Stergar
Keith Thomas

The Impalas is a Terre Haute band formed in 1959. They toured locally and nationally.

IMPALAS (1959)
Front row, left to right: Keith Thomas, Tom Stergar and Bill Pierce. Back row, left to right: Jim Padgett and Bill Lundwall

The Ink Spots

THE INK SPOTS

The Ink Spots were formed in the early 1930s in Indianapolis, Indiana. The original members were Orville "Happy" Jones, Ivory "Deek" Watson, Charlie Fuqua and the only Indiana native, Jerry Daniels. They were a popular vocal group that helped define the musical genre that led to Rhythm & Blues and rock and roll. They recorded on Victor and Decca Records and their first big hit, "If I Didn't Care," was released in 1939. They made many member changes through the years, but still retained the original Ink Spots sound. In 1989, they were inducted into the Rock and Roll Hall of Fame.

Johnny & The Pyramids

Group members include:

Danny Beach
Larry Deal
Jimmy (James) Elliott
Johnny Moore

Indianapolis doo-wop: group Johnny & The Pyramids was very popular on the teen scene. They performed at record hops and teen clubs with local disc jockeys. No recordings were made of Johnny & The Pyramids, but one member, Jimmy Elliott, later recorded a 45 single "Sheet Music"/"Touch and Go," on the American Sound label.

JOHNNY & THE PYRAMIDS (1959)
Back row, left to right: Larry Deal, Danny Beach and Jimmy Elliott.
Front: Johnny Moore.

Keetie & The Kats

Perhaps the most popular group working in Indianapolis during the 1950s and '60s was Keetie & The Kats. Keith Phillips (Keetie) was both a talented drummer and a showman. He possessed a special gift of gab that helped his band obtain some of the area's best bookings. In addition, Keetie enjoyed success in attracting the most talented musicians to his group. The old saying "Cats Have Nine Lives" fits Keetie & The Kats. Here's why!

1. The original Keetie &The Kats group formed around 1958. It included Keith Phillips on drums, Dave Ellman on piano

CONTINUED ON PAGE 28

KEETIE & THE KATS (1960)
Back row, left to right: Donny Sanders, Larry Lee, Keith Phillips and Dave Kellie. Front row: Bill Settles

KEETIE & THE KATS (1958)

Left to right: Larry Lee, Dave Ellman, Keith Phillips and Bill Rooker (Whiteland Barn)

LARRY LEE & KEITH PHILLIPS (1959)

and trumpet, Larry Lee on lead guitar, and Bill Rooker on rhythm guitar.

2. In 1959, guitarist Norm Shafey succeeded Bill Rooker.

3. In late 1959, Larry "Wazoo" Gardner, a local bass player, replaced Norm Shafey. Also joining the group was local saxman John Scott. and around the same time keyboardist Dave Kellie replaced Dave Ellman.

4. Bass player Bill Settles filled in for Larry Gardner in 1961 and saxophonist Donny Sanders replaced John Scott.

5. In 1962, Larry Lee left the group The Kats continued to tour as a four-piece ensemble under the name of Bill Black's Combo.

6. Guitarist Gary LeMaster joined the group around 1963 along with clarinetist Bob Snyder (formerly with Tommy Dorsey). The band changed its name to Keetie & The Kasuals and began to play more adult-oriented music, ranging from pop to Dixieland.

7. In 1964, Bob Snyder left the group and saxophonist Pete Funk and trombonist Jerry Woodward (from The Five Chords) were added.

8. In late 1964, the band changed its name to the Keith Phillips VI. Jerry Woodward left the group and Jesse Williams joined.

9. In 1965 or '66, Bruce Waterman and Skip Wagner joined the group. In 1967, The Keith Phillips IV broke up. The members scattered across the country

CONTINUED ON PAGE 29

KEETIE & THE KATS (1959)

Left to right: Larry Lee, John Scott, Norm Shafey, Larry Gardner, Dave Kellie
and Keith Phillips (drums).

Keetie & The Kats played the Whiteland Barn and other popular teen clubs in Indianapolis during the late 1950s and early '60s. Local singers that worked with Keetie's group during this time included Jimmy Clendening, Jerry Seifert and Dennis Turner. Recordings made by Keetie & The Kats include, "Move Part I & 2" (1960) on K-Records, and "Way Out"/"Crossties" (1962) on the Huron label.

David Lerchey (The Del Vikings)

Born in New Albany, Lerchey was baritone singer for the nationally known group The Del Vikings. This group became the first successful multi-racial rock 'n' roll band. The group became popular in 1957 with their smash hit, "Come Go With Me." It climbed to number four on the national charts. At that time, this was the highest position a song by a mixed-race group had achieved. One of Del Vikings later recordings, "Whispering Bells," was listed on the Billboard charts at number nine.

THE DEL VIKINGS
Kipp Johnson (top), Norman Wright (bottom),
center, left to right: Gus Bakus, Clarence Quick
and Dave Lerchey

Bobby Lewis

Bobby Lewis was born in Indianapolis on February 17, 1933. He began his career by selling pots for a traveling Indian. He also sang for a road show called *Bimbo's,* and then worked for funnyman Soupy Sales. Lewis' first recording around 1956 was taped in Chicago on the Parrot label. He then recorded "Mumbles Blues" for Spotlight Records. In 1958, Lewis moved to the Mercury label, with "Oh! Mr. Somebody." Three years later Lewis, recording for Beltone Records, broke through with his big hit "Tossin' And Turnin'." It was number one for seven weeks and became the most popular song of the year. Lewis returned to Indianapolis twice, once in 1962 to appear with the *Dick Clark Caravan of Stars* at the Indiana State Fairgrounds. Later he performed on the bandwagon for the Nixon administration. Bobby Lewis died April 28, 2020, at the age of 95.

BOBBY LEWIS

Jimmy Mack

Jimmy Mack (McDowell) was born in Lincoln, Nebraska. He moved to Indianapolis around 1957. He appeared on station WISH with his live *Teens 'N Tunes* radio show, His wife Peggy co-produced, and the dance program was top-rated. From 1957 until 1963, Jimmy was master of ceremonies for *Teen Twirl,* a popular television program on the Indianapolis station, WISH. That program featured live teen bands and singers similar to the popular *American Bandstand.* Jimmy Mack later hosted the television series, *Bandstand 13,* on Indianapolis station WLWI. Mack also appeared on other television and radio stations. He performed commercials for such shows as *Amos & Andy, The Mouseketeers,* and the *Annie Oakley*

CONTINUED ON PAGE 31

JIMMY MACK (1958)

show. Jimmy Mack lives in the Indianapolis area, where he is a successful photographer.

Lonnie Mack

Lonnie Mack (Lonnie Mcintosh) was born in Harrison, Indiana in 1941. He began playing professionally at an early age and worked in clubs and roadhouses around Indiana, Ohio and Kentucky. Famous for his Flying V Gibson guitar, Mack recorded many songs for King and Federal Records in Cincinnati. He played with R&B artists such as Hank Ballard, Freddie King and James Brown. In 1963, Lonnie recorded an instrumental version of Chuck Berry's hit, "Memphis" on Fraternity Records. It rose to number five on the charts. Other Mack recordings were "Wham!", "Where There's A Will There's A Way" and "Chicken Pickin." Lonnie Mack also made an appearance on the Doors *Morrison Hotel* album. He appeared with such major artists as Stevie Ray Vaughn, Bob Dylan, Mick Jagger and Paul Simon. He released his final album in 1990. Lonnie Mack passed away on April 21, 2016.

JIMMY MACK (1958)
Live on WISH television program, Teen Twirl.

LONNIE MACK BAND (1963)
Group members, not in order: Wayne Bullock, Truman Fields, Ron Grayson, Marv Lieberman, Irv Russotto and Lonnie Mack (far right).

No Witnesses

Group members include:

Gary Draper
Don Ellis
Doug Metcik
Doug Sterns
Jim Tutterow
Denny Wilson

Guitarist/leader Doug Sterns formed this group in the late 1950s. Sterns later re-united this group in the 1980s to perform on the nightclub circuit. The group was called Witness.

Paul Page

Paul Page was born in North Vernon, Indiana in 1910. He was a lifetime member of the Hollywood/LA musician's union and was a singer, pianoist, band director, artist, writer and composer. He published many albums and wrote hundreds of songs. Page worked for NBC radio in Chicago for 10 years. He conducted a Hawaiian big band throughout the Midwest and California and is a member of the Songwriters Hall of Fame. He loved Hawaiian music and played in Hawaii for many years. His most famous original song was "Kilroy Was Here" in 1946. Paul Page passed away in 1997.

The Playboys

Group members include:

Jerry Jaquess
Gary McKiern
Bill Roberts
Jim Spilker
Bill Vale
Gene Wheeler

This 1950s Indianapolis teen band was one of several groups that used the Playboys name.

Nooney "Everett" Rickett

Nooney Rickett was born in, Perry County, Kentucky. In the late 1950s, he lived in Indianapolis and attended Arsenal Technical High School. He recorded "Heaven On Earth"/"Trying to Forget" (1960) on MGM Records, and "Bye Bye Love"/"In The Swim" (1964) on 20th Century Fox. He later recorded on the Dimension, IT, and the Capitol labels. Nooney also made a guest appearance in a beach movie with Frankie Avalon and Annette Funicello. In 1958, Nooney could be seen at the Arsenal Grill across from Tech High School, slouched in a booth, strumming his guitar.

NOONEY "EVERETT" RICKETT

The Rockin Tones

Group members include:

Carl Junior Campbell
Darrel Wayne Chenowith
Jimmy Chenowith
Ray "Little Ray" Chenowith
Glen Westerfield

Rooker & The Rockers

Group members include:

Bill Rooker
Guy Tarrents
Dean Wagner

ROOKER & THE ROCKERS (1959)
Left to right: Guy Tarrents, Bill Rooker and Dean Wagner

The Rhythm Rockers

Group members include:

Johnny Bennett
George Carter
"Charlie Brown" Clark
Jim Crossen
Fred Lawson
Jack Scott

Jerry Seifert

JERRY SEIFERT (1958)

Indiana-born Jerry Seifert recorded his only local hit, "Dirty White Bucks"/"Never Baby Never" (1958) on Note Records. ABC-Paramount recording artist Ronnie Haig wrote both songs. In the mid-1980s, Jerry released another single, "Rockin' Fifties"/"My Love Just Ain't Getting Through" on the Sundial label.

The Shades

Group members include:

Jim Lorman
Jim Slack
John Tabor

Bill Sherrell

Bill Sherrell was born in Burkville, Kentucky, in 1929, and moved to Indianapolis at the age of six. From 1948 to 1950 he was a professional prize fighter. He played guitar and drums and performed in the local bars. Sherrell worked at the Roundup Bar for 12 years, playing music on stage and being a part-time bouncer.

He recorded some of Indiana's early rock 'n' roll recordings on the Tyme Records label. Released in 1958 and '59 were "Rock on Baby"/"Rock and Roll Teenager," "Teen Hop Rock"/"Cadillac Baby," "Kool Kat"/"Yes, No or Maybe" and "Don't You Rock Me Daddy-o"/"You're the Beat Within My Heart." All were recorded at the Chess Records studio in Chicago. Most of these recording were backed-up by the Dell Tones, and included Butch Nichols on guitar, Jim Eastman on piano and bass and Dickie Boles on drums. Now retired, in 2016 he was still living in Indianapolis at the age of 86.

BILL SHERRELL AND JERRY LEE LEWIS (1957)

Troy Shondell

Born in Fort Wayne, Troy Shondell (Gary Schelton) was an accomplished musician who attended Valparaiso University. While majoring in music in 1961, he recorded and produced a song titled, "This Time." He released it on his own label, Gold Crest. Liberty Records learned of the song and Shondell re-recorded it for their label. It zoomed to success, climbing to number six on the top Billboard 100 and remained there for twelve weeks. Troy Shondell died on January 7, 2016 at the age of 76.

The Showmen

THE SHOWMEN (1957)

Group members include:

Walt Reed
Doug Sterns
Jerry Thompson
Jim Tutterow
Buddy Van Osdol
Gil Work

Other members were:

Jack Aldrich
Steve Smith
Dave Thompson

THE CROWNS, LIVE AT THE WESTLAKE BEACH CLUB (1958)
Members included John Bennett, Larry Goshen, Jack Scott, Bill Stewart, Gary Thaxton and Dick Walters

The Sounds Of The Crowns

The Indianapolis-based band Sounds of the Crowns never recorded under this name. They had released an earlier single under the name of Jerry Lee Williams & The Crowns, recorded on the Solid Gold label. This group was quite popular with the teens, playing record hops with disc

CONTINUED ON PAGE 37

jockeys "Bouncin' Bill" Baker and Jim Shelton. They also appeared at Westlake and the Whiteland Barn.

Nancee South

Terre Haute native Nancee South was a singer, organist and dancer. She toured with the McGuire Sisters and Julius LaRosa. Nancee won the *Arthur Godfrey's talent Scouts Show* in 1957, and later appeared on *Jerry Van Dyke's Variety Show*. South passed away in 1999.

The Spaniels

Group members include:

Opal Cortney, Jr.
Gerald Gregory
James "Pookie" Hudson
Willis C. Jackson

Later members were:
James Cochran, Donald Porter,
Carl Rainge and **Lester Williams**

This singing group from Gary first performed together at Roosevelt High School around 1953. Their initial recording, "Baby Its You," was performed on the Chance label, later known as Vee Jay Records. The Spaniels were the first group to be signed by the Vee Jay label. Their first hit occurred in 1954 with "Goodnite Sweetheart, Goodnite." Other recordings included, "You Painted Pictures" (1955), "You Gave Me Peace Of Mind" (1956), "Everyone's Laughing" (1957), "Stormy Weather" (1958), and "I Know" (1960).

PHOTO CREDIT: HERBERT GOSHEN

LARRY GOSHEN (1958)

Left to right: Ben Falber Jr., Jerry Van Dyke, Joseph Benti and Nancee South (1957)

The Turbans

Group members include:

Bob Bernard

Charence Dorsey

Tony Goodrich

Hilton Hudson

Herman Lewis

This group was formed in 1957. It was re-formed by singer Bob Bernard and re-titled The Monograms. In the 1960s, The Monograms became one of the top soul acts in Indiana. (See Monograms, in the Nightclub section.)

Whiteland Barn

The Whiteland Barn was one of the hottest teen dance clubs around the Indianapolis area in the '50s and '60s. Owned and operated by Don Hohlt, it was the fun place to go on Sunday nights. The Barn was located 20 miles from Indianapolis on Front Road, amidst the farmland of Whiteland, Indiana. The Barn opened sometime around 1958 and was hosted by WIBC radio personalities Bouncin' Bill Baker and Jack Morrow. Besides being a local venue for bands like Keetie & The Kats, The Dawnbeats and others, it revealed an unusual showroom for National entertainers. It was a large barn with restrooms/snack bar downstairs and a small stage and large dance floor in the upstairs loft. Some of the national acts to perform at the Barn were Jerry Lee Lewis, Duane Eddy, The Ventures, Roy Orbison, Neil Sedaka, The Beach Boys, Brenda Lee, Fats Domino, Bo Diddley, the Drifters and many others. After closing in the late sixties, the Barn was destroyed by fire.

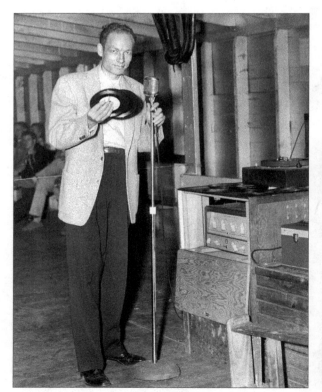

JACK MORROW (1950'S)
WIBC disc jockey at the Whiteland Barn

Bob Pence & The Rhythm Rangers (First band to play the Whiteland Barn with the first poster) 1958?

Jerry Lee Williams & The Crowns

Group members include:

Larry Goshen
Bill Stewart
Gary Thaxton
Dick Walters
Jerry Lee Williams

Formed in 1959, and together for only a short time, this group recorded "The Go Tune/Wibcee" (1959), on Solid Gold Records. "Wibcee" became a popular recording, but was short-lived because of its title and the fact that it was only played on WIBC Radio. Due to a disagreement between Williams and the other members, he was replaced by guitarist Jack Scott. The group then became The Sounds of The Crowns. Jerry Williams died on May 22, 2015 at the age of 81.

JERRY LEE WILLIAMS & THE CROWNS (1958)
Left to right: Larry Goshen, Bill Stewart, Jerry Williams, Dick Walters
and Gary Thaxton

Tommy Wills

TOMMY WILLS

Tommy Wills was born in Middletown, Ohio. He moved to Indianapolis in 1971. Wills learned the guitar at the age of eight. After entering junior high, he switched to saxophone. Wills made several recordings in the mid-1950s. Some have become collector's items. Wills recorded on the Club Miami label. In 1954, he recorded a song titled, "Let 'Em Roll" featuring singer Marti Maes. That recording is valued in the $250 price range and sought after in the collector's market. In 1961, Wills recorded under the name The Tomcats and released a single on Terry Records. In 1963, he hit the national charts with his instrumental recording of "Man With A Horn." It was released on Gregory Records. Wills has toured the United States and Canada, performing everything from country and swing to rock n' roll. After moving to Indianapolis, he performed on the Holiday Inn circuit. In the 1980s, he directed the Ted Weems Orchestra. Wills later directed the Eddy Howard Orchestra. In 1989, he toured with Bill Haley's Comets. Wills released two CDs, *Swingin' The Blues,* a recording with the big band sound, and a Christmas CD, *Happy Holidays.* Tommy Wills died on December 14, 2017 at the age of 76.

Dale Wright

DALE WRIGHT (1959)

Dale Wright, who was an Ohio native, performed with some of Indiana's top bands including Keetie & The Kats, the Dawnbeats and The Crowns. His recording of "She's Neat" (1958) on Fraternity Records climbed to the #39 position on the Billboard charts. Wright made guest appearances on *American Bandstand* and *The Merv Griffin Show.* He also performed as a character actor for the national network series of *The Rifleman.* Dale Wright died in April of 2007.

Al "Alphonso" Young

Alphonso Young was born in Louisville, Kentucky. He moved to Indianapolis in 1959. A guitarist, he performed with The Presidents and appeared at George's Place on Indiana Avenue. In 1962, Young left for Clarksville to join guitarist Jimi Hendrix. They formed a group called The King Casuals. In 1963, Hendrix moved the group to Nashville and Al returned to Indianapolis. Young continued to perform with the Presidents and other local bands. Members of the Presidents include Louis Cochran, Harold Elery, Leroy Massey, and Mr. "T," Howard O'Brook, Phillip Slaughter and Al Young.

AL "ALPHONSO" YOUNG

JIMI HENDRIX & AL YOUNG (1950S)

AMOS ARTHUR (1950s)

Proprietor of Arthur's Music Store, Fountain Square, Indianapolis. Arthur's Music Store was founded in 1952 by Amos Arthur and is still in operation today at the same location. It is now owned and operated by his daughter Linda Osborne and granddaughter Amy England.

The Sensational Sixties

Indianapolis Teen Tempo *July magazine cover*
and Poster of Three Star Promotions for Sir Winston & The Commons

The Sensational Sixties

When John F. Kennedy was elected President of the United States in 1960, the country was as optimistic as his smile. Three years later, he would be assassinated. A year prior to his death, Cuba nearly caused a world war by permitting the Soviet Union to base missiles on its shores. When Nikita Khrushchev backed down, the world was saved from potential extinction.

As the decade progressed, civil rights became the call of the wild. Riots in the south were met with determination by Dr. Martin Luther King and his followers. An assassin's bullet in 1968 ended his crusade. That year John Kennedy's brother, Robert, a presidential aspirant, suffered the same fate at the hands of Sirhan Sirhan.

By the end of the decade, the nation had witnessed the surreal musical happening at Woodstock and the amazing achievement of Neil Armstrong landing on the moon. The Chicago Seven trial was held. Abbie Hoffman and company became front-page news.

Cultural events besides Woodstock included the penning of *One Flew Over the Cuckoo's Nest* by Ken Kesey. An art exhibit by pop artist Andy Warhol featured his Campbell's Soup can, and the first James Bond film, *Goldfinger,* highlighted the New York film scene.

The Sensational Sixties marked a revolution in modern music. The decade featured the evolution, among others, of the Beatles, the Rolling Stones, the Beach Boys, and crooner Roy Orbison. The Temptations, the Four Tops, and Ruby and the Romantics were favorites. Ed Sullivan's television program was a must-see.

Popular songs of the '60s included, "Cathy's Clown," "The Twist," "Go Away Little Girl," "Last Train to Clarksville," and "Aquarius." The Beatles entertained the world with "Hard Day's Night," "Eleanor Rigby," "I Want To Hold Your Hand," and many others.

Indiana-born or Indiana-based musicians played their part in the rock revolution, but they also contributed to the soul and jazz scene. Young people in the '60s congregated at the Flame Club, the House of Sound, the Pink Panther, the Speckled Axe, the Tiger-A-Go-Go, and Party Time. Jim Shelton and Bill Baker continued to be popular disc jockeys, as did Tom Mathis, Reb Porter, and Jay Reynolds.

Teenagers kept up to date with developments in the rock arena through monthly publications. The most popular was *Teen Tempo*, an Indianapolis publication that provided local rock groups with visibility.

In every nook and cranny, "garage bands" emerged during the '60s. That connotation was unfortunate since the bands were creative and popular. Many gained fame despite their being laughed at for rehearsing in garages.

Across Indiana, the blend of rock, soul, and jazz provided a perfect mix for music lovers. The musicians and groups that follow contributed to a time when the listening was easy during ***The Sensational Sixties.***

The Aquanauts

Group members include:

Dan Botnich

Steve Harding

Tom Harding

Lee Morrell

Wally Murphy

This Indianapolis band released two singles, "Rumble On The Docks" and "High Divin'" (1963), on Safari Records.

Baby Huey & The Babysitters

Baby Huey (James Ramey) was born in Richmond, Indiana in 1944. He performed in the early '60s with his band the Babysitters, playing R&B and later a more psychedelic brand of soul. Ramey had a weight problem and weighed from 350 to 400 pounds. He recorded one single on Curtom Records titled "Listen to Me" in 1962. One of the early members of his group was singer Chaka Khan. Baby Huey (Ramey) died October 28, 1970.

BABY HUEY & THE BABYSITTERS

The Backdoor Men

Group members include:

Fred Hostetter

Steve Kreidear

Dean Taggard

From Elkhart, Indiana, this group recorded one 45, "Evil"/"Corinna" (1969), on the Fujimo label.

BOYS NEXT DOOR (1965)

The Boys Next Door

Group members include:

Jim Adams

Skeet Bushor

Steve Drybread

Jim Koss

Steve Lester

Originally called The Four Wheels, this Indianapolis group changed its name around 1965 to The Boys Next Door. They produced several recordings, "Why Be Proud"/"Suddenly She Was Gone" (1965), on Soma Records, "There Is No Great Sin"/"I Could See Me Dancing With You" (1966), on Cameo Records, and "The Wildest Christmas"/"Christmas Kiss" (1966), on the Bad label.

Roy Chaney

Bass player Roy Chaney was born in Indianapolis in 1948. He performed with the psychedelic group The Count Five. This group recorded "Psychotic Reaction" (1966), on the Double Shot label. The recording reached the number five spot on the Billboard charts.

Chances 'R

Group members include:

Steve Fossen

Allen Kirsch

Ron Rutjes

Chris Skillman

Larry Streuber

This band hailed from Chesterton. They produced one recording, "I'll Have You Crying"/"Winds and Sea" (1965) on the Quill label.

The Checkmates, Ltd.

Group members include:

Sonny Charles
Marvin Smith
Robert Stevens
Harvey Trees
William Van Buskirk

The Checkmates were formed in 1957 in Fort Wayne. They were one of the first racially mixed ensembles and made their first recording on the Chicago based I.R.P. label in 1963. In 1969, they recorded "Black Pearl," produced by Phil Spector on the A&M label. It climbed to number thirteen on the Billboard charts and remained in the Top 100 for ten weeks. After a short, inactive period during the early 1970s, leader Sonny Charles re-formed the group. It became successful in Las Vegas and has won several awards for Best Lounge Act. Charles later became a singer for the Steve Miller Band.

THE CHECKMATES, LTD.
Left to right: Bill Van Buskirk, Sonny Charles, Marvin Smith, Harvey Trees and Bobby Stevens

The Chosen Few

THE CHOSEN FEW (1967)
Left to right: Steve Nephew, John Cascella. Carl Storie, Jack "Happy Jack" Hamilton, Richie Berman and Haji Baba

Group members include:

Dave Barnes
Dave Bennett
John Cascella
Jack Hamilton
Carl Storie

This band recorded several singles on the Denim label in the mid-1960s, and one LP, *The Chosen Few* (1969), on RCA. Around 1972, they formed a group called Limousine, and recorded one self-titled album on the GSF label. Less than a year later, they created the popular group, The Faith Band. The original members of this group (shown in the 1967 photo) included Haji Baba, Richie Berman and Steve Nephew.

The Cirkit

Group members include:

Scott Glemsiecke
Dave Goldman
Bruce Hainey
Rod Hansen
Mike Richards
Jim Shindell

This Michigan City-based group recorded one single "Yesterday We Laughed"/"I Was Wrong" (1967), on Unicorn Records.

Coven

Group members include:

Jinx Dawson
Greg "Oz" Osborne
Steve Ross
Dave Wilkerson

In 1968, the Indianapolis group Coven recorded their first album, *Witchcraft,* for Mercury Records. Since the name Coven denoted an assembly of witches, the group's music was banned in Detroit. In the late 1970s, Coven hit the charts with "One Tin Soldier" from the movie soundtrack of *Billy Jack.* They recorded two other albums

COVEN (1968)
Left to right: Dave Wilkerson. Jinx Dawson, Steve Ross and Greg "Oz" Osborne

under the Coven name, *Coven* on MGM Records in 1971, and *Blood On The Snow* on Buddah Records in 1974. Other members of the Coven group were John Hobbs, David Larman and Chris Neilsen. As of 2018, Jinx reformed the Coven band and is touring Sweden, Germany and other points across the world.

The Dawn Five

Group members include:

Steve Benham
Dave Dunne
Dave Mckown
Greg Nicoloff
Mike Nicoloff

The Dawn Five from Indianapolis opened for such national acts as The Turtles and Sonny & Cher. They recorded one single "A Necessary Evil"/"Mike's Bag" (1965), on the Bee Gee label.

THE DAWN FIVE

The Endd

Group members include:

Larry Anderson
Russ Sanders

This La Porte group recorded several singles in the mid-1960s. They included "So Sad"/"Emancipation" (1965), "Project Blue"/"Out Of My Hands" (1966), "Don't It Make You Feel Like Crying"/"Gonna Send You Back To Your Mother" (1966), and "Come On In To My World"/"This Is The Zoo, Plus Two" (1966). All were recorded on the Seascape label.

The Four Wheels

Group members include:

Jim Adams
Skeet Bushor
Steve Drybread
Jim Koss
Steve Lester

The Four Wheels preceded the popular Indianapolis group The Boys Next Door. They recorded one single, "Central High Playmate"/"Cold 45" (1964), on the Soma label.

Denise L. Grissom

Denise Grissom

Larry Goshen

DENISE GRISSOM

Indianapolis-born Denise Grissom began performing as a vocalist at the age of thirteen. After graduating from Shortridge High School, Denise continued entertaining in the 1960s by working with the all-female group The Pearls. She later performed with many national and regional acts, including recording artist Stevie Wonder. Denise continued to perform in the Indianapolis jazz circuit with drummer Dick Dickinson.

The Heavy

Group members include:

Larry Ingle
Phil Thompson
Frankie Watters
Jeff Williams

This Kokomo-based group was known for their wild clothes and equally wild stage antics. Guitarist and singer Phil Thompson later performed under the name of Phil T. Blues and made several recordings. (See 1990s).

THE HEAVY (1968)
Left to right: Larry Ingle, Phil Thompson, Frankie Watters and Jeff Williams

Billy Henderson (The Spinners)

Singer Billy Henderson was born on August 9, 1939 in Indianapolis, Indiana. In 1954, Henderson joined James Edward, Henry Fambrough, Pervis Jackson and C.P. Spencer in the group Domingoes. In 1961 they replaed Edwards with Bobby Smith and changed their name to The Spinners. Their first hit recording in 1961 was "That is What Girls Are Made For" on Tri-Phi Records. In 2004, Henderson was dismissed from the group for suing the group's business manager to obtain financial records. Billy Henderson, one of the original members of The Spinners, died on Feburary 2, 2007 of complications from diabetes.

JOHN EDWARDS   HENRY FAMBROUGH   BILLY HENDERSON   BOBBIE SMITH   PERVIS JACKSON
THE SPINNERS

THE SPINNERS

Hickory Wind

Group members include:

Alan Jones
Mike McGuyer
Bobby Strehl

This Evansville group recorded one album titled, *Hickory Wind* (1969) on the Gigantic record label. Only 100 copies were pressed, making this record highly collectible. Prices range from $500 to $1,000 per album. This band preceded the B.F. Trike Band. They recorded an album for RCA in 1971 that was never released.

The Highlighters

THE HIGHLIGHTERS

Group members include:

Richard "Boola" Ball
James Boone
James Brantley
James "Porkchop" Edwards
Clifford Palmer

(Later members)

James Bell
Dewane Garvin

The Highlighters were formed in the early 1960s. They re-formed around 1968 with singer James Bell and drummer Dewane "Funky Buzzard" Garvin. This band played the local nightclub circuit. In 1969, they recorded the regional hit, "Poppin' Popcorn," on the Rojam label. They later recorded a James Bell original titled, "The Funky 16 Corners," released on the Three Diamonds label. The Highlighters members changed, but they made five more recordings before disbanding. They recorded on the Three Diamonds, Chess and Lulu labels.

Him Her & Them

Group members include:

Bob Dawson

Jinx Dawson

Steve Farber

Greg Johnson

David Larman

Greg Osborne

Formed in 1964 in Indianapolis, two members of this group (Jinx Dawson & Greg Osborne) later became part of Coven. (See Coven, 1960s)

Ice

Ice was a popular Indianapolis rock band from the 1960s. Members were Barry Crawford, Jim Lee, Mike Saligoe, John Schafer and Rich Strange.

The Idle Few

Group members include:

Ron Benneth

Ron Knoop

Dan McLean

Paul Romine

Rick Webster

Originally called The Kings Men (1958), they changed their name to The Idle Few. The group performed with such artists as the Beach Boys, the Byrds, the Supremes, and Bobby Goldsboro. They recorded "Another World"/"Farmer John" (1966) on Suma, and the single "Letter to Santa"/"Splishin & Splashin" (1967).

THE IDLE FEW (1962)

The Jackson 5 (The Jacksons)

Group members include:

Jackie Jackson
Jermaine Jackson
Marlon Jackson
Michael Jackson
Tito Jackson

The Jackson brothers were born in Gary, Indiana. Their father Joe, a guitarist with his own R&B band, The Falcons, provided musical training. Michael was not an original member of the group the Jackson Family Singers. It consisted of brothers Jackie, Tito, and Jermaine. Michael and brother Marlon later joined to form The Jackson 5.

The group first started performing in clubs around 1962. Their first recording was on the Indiana based label Steeltown. They auditioned for Motown in 1968, and made their first recording, "I Want You Back" a year later. It was the fastest selling recording in the company's history.

After many successful recordings with Motown, the contract expired in 1975 and The Jackson 5 signed with EPIC records. After losing a lawsuit filed by Motown regarding the rights to the name The Jackson 5, they became known as The Jacksons.

Royal Jones and The Dukes

Group members include:

Gary Jones
Gene Jones
Keith Kilmer
Mike Kiser
Jay Purvis
Skip Walters
Dave Workman

Royal Jones and the Dukes was an early 1960s band from Goshen that recorded on Fujimo and a Chicago based label titled Signett.

THE JACKSON 5

Joys of Life

JOYS OF LIFE (1967)
Front row, left to right: Jeff Mills, Corky Kirk and Danny McMullin. Middle row: Craig Gardener and Jim Albrecht. Third row: Jeff McMullin

Group members include:

Jim Albrecht
Craig Gardener
Corky Kirk
Danny McMullin
Jeff McMullin
Jeff Mills

In 1967, this Indianapolis group recorded "Good Times Are Over"/"Descent," a 45 single on Columbia Records. Recording on a national label was a great achievement for a local group, but the song was not a national success. Bill Overman, a local producer who helped many other bands achieve local success, produced this recording. In the 1990s, musician Jim Albrecht opened a recording studio. He performed with such groups as Small Talk, Trinia & The Gypsies, and many others.

The Knightsmen

THE KNIGHTSMEN

Group members include:

Darrell Ball	**Karl Hinkle**
Gary Irwin	**David Lee**
Donald Lee	**Rob McCoy**
Tom Rea	**Mark Tribby**

Formed in 1965, this Indianapolis band recorded one single, "Gimme Some Kinda Sign"/"Let Love Come Between Us." The Knightsmen disbanded around 1968.

Singer Karl Hinkle later became a member of the popular Wright Brothers band. (See Wright Brothers, 1970s)

The Lords of London

Group members include:

Harry Cangany
Marty Lambert
Mike Lekse
Richie Medvescek
Frank Wechsler

Formed in 1965, this Indiana band made two recordings, "Broken Heart of C.O.D."/"Sit Down And Dance" (1965), on the Domain label, and "Time Waits For No One"/"Cornflakes And Ice Cream" (1966) on Decca.

The Lost Souls

Group members include:

Danny Dain
Charlie Hinkle
John Moore
Phil Thompson
Dave Trueblood

This Kokomo band was formed in 1967. They performed across Indiana.

The McCoys

Group members include:

Randy Hobbs
Bobbie Peterson
Randy Zehringer
Rick Zehringer

This Indiana and Ohio-based group was formed in Union City, Indiana, in 1962. The McCoys became famous three years later with their Bang Records recording of "Hang On Sloopy." Another top ten entry was a sound-alike version of "Sloopy" titled, "Fever." The group disbanded in 1969. Later, guitarist Rick Zehringer (second from left) changed his last name to Derringer. In 1973, he joined the popular Edgar Winters band.

THE McCOYS (1965)
Left to right: Randy Zehringer, Rick Zehringer, (DJ) Bob Berry , Bob Peterson and Randy Hobbs

Me And Them Guys

Group members include:

Marty Baker
Rod Kersey
Steve Michael
Steve Pritchard
Craig Terry

High school students from Greencastle formed this band. The group was popular in local teen clubs and performed regularly at Purdue University. They recorded one single in 1965, "I Love Her So"/"Somethin' Else" on the Grette label.

Keith Murphy & Daze

KEITH MURPHY & DAZE
Front row, left to right: Bill Shearer and Keith Murphy. Back row, left to right: Phil Fosnough, Jerry Asher and John Asher.

Group members include:

Jerry Asher
John Asher
Phil Fosnough
Keith Murphy
Bill Shearer

This rock group from the Marion area was formed in 1964. It released one single on the King label. It was one of the last recordings pressed on King before the death of owner Sid Nathan. Due to his death, only 100 copies were produced, making this recording valuable for record collectors. Valued in the $1,000 price range is "Slightly Reminiscent Of Her"/"Dirty Ol' Sam" (1968) on King. Singer and guitarist Keith Murphy also recorded an earlier local hit "Cindy Lou"/"Little Loved One" (1963) on the Stacy label. That was under the name of Keith O'Connor. It also featured the group The Torkays.

The Outsiders

Group members include:

Dan Hailey
Mike Ray
Rob Sweeney
Wayne Wilson

This Indianapolis band claimed to be associated with national recording artists, The Outsiders. They recorded "Time Won't Let Me" in 1966. Even though this group toured under the Outsiders name, none of these members performed on the original recording.

The Reflections

This group from Indianapolis recorded a regional hit in 1963 titled "In the Still of The Night"/"Tic Toc," on the Tigre Records label. Members were Perry "Pat" Baldwin, Larry Dunlap, Dave Dunn and Chuck Tunnah. Some of the Reflections became members of the California band Stark Naked & The Car Thieves.

THE REFLECTIONS
Left to right: Chuck Tunnah, Dave Dunn, Perry (Pat) Baldwin and Larry Dunlap.

Rivieras

Group members include:

Paul Dennert
Marty Fortson
Doug Gean
Otto Nuss
Joe Pennell

This band, originally called The Playmates, did not originate in California as some might assume but in South Bend, Indiana. The Rivieras achieved much commercial success in the 1960s with their hit recording of "California Sun." It climbed to the number five spot on the Billboard charts. They later recorded two lesser hits, "Let's Have A Party" and "Rockin' Robin." In 1964, the Rivieras recorded two LPs, *Campus Party* for Riviera (701) and *Let's Have A Party* on the USA (102) label.

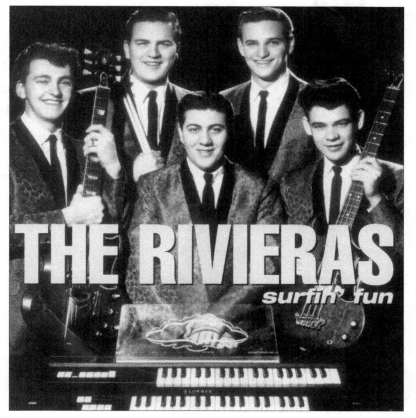

THE RIVIERAS

Ronnie & The Rascals

This band from the 1960s played mostly top 40 R&B. They performed in the Indianapolis area, working in teen clubs such as the House of Sounds, Westlake and the Whiteland Barn. Original members were Ronnie Blackstone, Bob Brown, Lanny Lambert, Mike Quick and Rick Wilheim.

RONNIE & THE RASCALS

The Sentimentals

This classic Motown-style duo was formed in Indianapolis in 1962. Touring the United States, The Sentimentals opened for such artists as Chuck Jackson, Patti LaBelle & The Blue Belles, Little Anthony & The Imperials, Martha & The Vandellas, and The Marevelettes. They performed from 1962 through 1970 and recorded one single "I Know You Too Well"/"Now Is Here" (1970), on the Naptown label.

THE SENTIMENTALS (1968)
Josephine Terrell and Henry Hinch

The Sangralads

Group members include:

Phil Armstrong
Mike Biddle
Aaron Burnell
Rick Ingle

The Sangralads were formed in 1966 at the Sangralea Valley Boys Home in Logansport. The group made exclusive tours of the United States and performed locally at clubs such as Indiana Beach. They also appeared on the *Jim Gerard Show.* Their recordings include, "Mary's Kid"/"Think Of What You're Saying" (1968), and "Quasar 45"/"There Must Be Light" (1969), on the Whap Record label.

The Shy Ones

Group members include:

Bonnie McDowell
Robin McDowell
Barb Gabriel
Carol Buckoski
Jeanne Schuller
Sandy Gay

THE MACK SISTERS

THE SHY ONES (1968)

This all-female band was formed in Indianapolis in 1968. The Shy Ones were quite popular on the college circuit, performing at many local fraternities. During the Vietnam War, they entertained at Fort Harrison and Bonnie and Robin performed for the troops overseas under the name of the Mack Sisters. The two McDowell sisters later formed the popular Indiana show group, Five Easy Pieces. (See Five Easy Pieces 1970s)

Sir Winston & The Commons

Group members include:

Don Basore
Herbie Crawford
Ronnie Matelic
Johnny Medvescek
Joe Stout

This Indiana group was very popular with teenagers. In 1966, they opened for the Byrds at the Indianapolis Coliseum. They recorded two singles, "Come Back Again"/"We're Gonna Love" (1965) on Soma Records, and "Not The Spirit Of India"/"One Last Chance" (1967) on Nauseating Butterfly.

Sounds Unlimited

Group members include:

Phil Brandt
Steve Foster
Ken Mahlke
Wayne Wilson

Sounds Unlimited was very popular in the mid-1960s. They played in teen clubs such as Westlake, Indiana Roof, Flame Club, the Pink Panther and the Whiteland Barn. They opened for national groups like the McCoys, Byrds and Mitch Ryder and the Detroit Wheels. Two later members, Terry Talbot and John Talbot, formed the 1970s rock group, Mason Profit. Sounds Unlimited recorded one single. "A Girl As Sweet As You" (1967), on the Dunwich Records label.

SOUNDS UNLIMITED (1966)

Stark Naked & The Car Thieves

Some of the original members of this band were derived from the AristCats and Reflection groups in Indianapolis. They became popular in the late 1960s and early '70s performing in the California area. They made many recordings, and some that made the National Billboard Chart. Original members were Micky Borden, Mac Brown, Larry Dunlap, Dave Dunn, Les Silvey and Leonard Souza.

Jerry Thompson

Drummer Jerry Thompson was born in Indianapolis on April 11, 1944. He performed with the Showmen band in 1957 and continued to play the drums with many groups throughout the years. In the mid-1960s he was drummer for the Hollywood Argyles, the famous "Alley Oop" band. This group included singer Sharon Reni, Bobby Rey, Gary LeMaster, Jerry Thompson and Bill Fliehman. It was one of many groups that used the Argyles name for road work. Thompson recorded with the Melting Pot band in 1971 on the Ampex Record Label. Jerry Thompson passed away on July 29, 2012.

SHARON RENI AND THE HOLLYWOOD ARGYLES
Left to right: Sharon Reni, Bobby Rey, Gary LeMaster, Jerry Thompson and Bill Fliehman

The Tikis

Group members include:

Bob Folger
Dave Webster
Rick Workman
Pat Wo

A band formed in Syracuse around 1966.

The Torkays

THE TORKAYS
Left to right: Keith Murphy, Jim Aguilar, Rocky Hall and Frank Aguilar

Group members include:

Frank Aguilar
Jim Aguilar
Rocky Hall
Keith Murphy (O'Connor)
Richie Niverson

The popular group from Marion and Sweetser performed in the early 1960s at Indiana Beach and at local teen dances. Their release of "Karate" (1963) was the premiere recording of any martial arts theme. "Karate"/"I Don't Like It" was released on the Stacy label. The Torkays featured Keith O'Connor. He also recorded "Cindy Lou"/"Little Loved One" on the Stacy label. It was released around the same time.

Junior Walker

JUNIOR WALKER

(Autry DeWalt)

Saxophonist Junior Walker, born Autry DeWalt, in Blythesville, Arkansas, spent his teenage years at a high school in South Bend. In Indiana, he coined the name Junior Walker and formed his first band, The Jumping Jacks. After graduating from high school, Junior played in local jazz and R&B clubs. In the late 1950s, he moved to Battle Creek, Michigan. There he formed Junior Walker & The All Stars and began his professional recording career. Walker was one of Motown's most popular artists. He recorded many charted hits. Some of Junior Walker's most popular recordings include "Shotgun" (1965), "Shake and Fingerpop" (1965), "How Sweet It Is (to be loved by you)" (1966), and his first vocal recording "What Does It Take (to win your love)" (1969). Junior Walker died of cancer in Battle Creek on November 25, 1995.

Front Row—Tom Mathis, Chuck Browning, Bill Donnella, Jay Reynolds, Bob Lyons. Back Row—T. J. Byers, Dick Saint, Reb Porter, Don Lancer, Ron Jackson, Ron Hofer.

WIFE DISC JOCKEYS

The XL's

Group members include:

Ted Benneth

G.C. Egy

Bill Evans

Tim Ferguson

Greg Funk

This mid-1960s band was from Terre Haute.

Other 1960s Notables

Astronauts

Billy Day

Becki Holland

Dick Dewayne

Dick Summer

Dick York

Doug Stauch

Fabulous Jokers

Harry Maginity

Jan Sanders

Jim & Dan Bowlin

John Harding

Kapris

Mike Clark

Rick Fortune

Ron Bonham

Runner Whitten

Shadows of Sound

Steve Baker

The Cardinals

The Chordells

The Illusions

The Impacts

The Jiants

The Juveniles

The Noblemen

The Nocturnes

The Ramrods

The Reflections

The Royal Vikings

The Untouchables

The Vendettas

The Wild Things

Tiny Vee

Vegas

Walter "Arkie" Bittle

Young Set

Nightclubs, Bars & Music Stars of the Sixties

Indianapolis in the 60's

fabulous
B.G. Ramblers
FROM N.Y. & ROUNDTABLE
AND MIAMI'S PEPPERMINT LOUNGE

TUESDAYS - "TWIST" CONTEST
WEDNESDAYS - "LADIES' NIGHT"
THURSDAYS - "LIMBO" NIGHT
EVERY SATURDAY
JAM SESSION - 3-6 P.M.

the **HOLLYOKE** Club
3901 E. WASH. ST.
PLENTY OF FREE PARKING !

Oscar's
BOOM BOOM Room
1435 COMMERCE
ME 7-0536
Presents
the **FIVE CHORDS**
FOR YOUR DANCING
AND LISTENING
PLEASURE

JAM SESSION!
SATURDAYS 3-6 P.M.

the **SCARLETS**
ONE OF THE NATION'S
MOST VERSATILE
MUSICAL-VOCAL
COMEDY GROUPS
★
ENTERTAINMENT
DANCING
★
THE CITY'S
LARGEST
DANCE
FLOOR!

NICK and **JERRY'S**
1110 N. MERIDIAN
ME 5-0563

Hi... I'm Sam

...at the carrousel

COCKTAIL HOUR PRICES 5-7 P.M.
Count Fisher Eve Rene' trio
the twisting
carrousel kittens
2162 N. Meridian
WA 3-0661

CARROUSEL

PINK POODLE
the Showplace
of Indiana
presents

get set for
a laff riot!

"THE
FUNNIEST
MAN IN
THE
WORLD"

redd foxx

MATINEES
SAT.
4-7 P.M.

Pink Poodle
252 N. CAPITOL
ME 2-0087

DANCING
ENTERTAINMENT
TWISTING
NIGHTLY
WITH
THE ORIGINAL
DUKES

the **LEMON TWIST**
1116 PROSPECT
(IN FOUNTAIN SQUARE)
ME 5-0548

Let's **Twist!**
at the most talked
about club in Indpls!
featuring the LOUNGE TWISTERS
+ SCREAMIN' JIMMY
and the swinging DUKES band!
Hilarious Twist Shows
...the audience participating

Peppermint Lounge
of Indianapolis
(RAIL CLUB)

MaD, MaD, MaD SHOW!

SEE AND HEAR THE   DANCE TO & LISTEN TO

Nightclubs, Bars, & Music Stars of the Sixties

There's something special about a darkened room, the lighted stage, and the moment when a musical act is introduced to wild applause causing the heartbeat to flutter. Nightclubs and bars are the melting pot of music where fans and musicians alike gather to meet, greet, and enjoy live music.

During the 1960s, Indiana featured a plethora of mystical venues to the delight of those that believe live music is better, or at least as good as sex. They included The Embers, the Towne House, and the Carousel. Others were Nick & Jerrys, Dan-T Supper Club, the Holyoke, Tic Toc and the Rail Club. It was later known as the Peppermint Lounge.

Great jazz and soul clubs included the Pink Poodle, where Jimmy Smith and Arthur Prysock performed, and the Barrington Lounge. It featured the Jimmy Coe Trio with Melvin Rhyne performing on the B-3 organ, and Sonny Johnson on drums. At the Holyoke, the sounds of Billy day, Wayne Cochran and the immortal Buddy Rich filtered through the smoke-filled room. Other musicians of note include:

The Accents

Group members include:

Dick Donahue
Ron Russell
Vince Sanders

The Accents were a very popular trio from the Indianapolis area. They performed on the nightclub circuit and were noted for their smooth harmony. They recorded four albums, *Full Spectrum* on Forward Records, *Yesterday Today, and a Touch of Tomorrow* on RCA, and *Next Bus South* and *Two Sides of the Accents,* on Entertainer Records.

THE ACCENTS
Left to right: Ron Russell, Dick Donahue and Vince Sanders

ANDY ANDERSON & THE JETS
Front row, left to right: (unidentified) and Jimmy Ganzberg.
Back row, left to right: Ralph Coverstone, Andy Anderson and Don Higgs.

Marden Baker Quintet

MARDEN BAKER QUINTET #2
Left to right: Larry Goshen, Rondo Loschky, Gary Thaxton, Jimmy Ganzberg and Marden Baker

Group members include:

Marden Baker
Larry Goshen
Jack Scott
Bill Stewart
Gary Thaxton

This quintet performed a jazz-rock sound and entertained in many top nightspots in Indianapolis. This group was originally called The Sounds Of The Crowns. They changed their name to better fit the nightclub circuit. The group performed floor-shows, backing up such acts as the Cavaliers, Monograms and Gary Wells. Headlining the group was tenor saxophonist Marden Baker. This group, later known as the Marden Baker Quartet, performed around 1960 at one of the popular jazz clubs on Indiana Avenue. Later members included Jim Ganzberg and Ron Loschky.

The Blue Tones

THE BLUE TONES (1961)
From bottom to top: Danny Ornung, Myron Murry, Mickey Kirkpatrick and Jimmy Theros

Group members include:

Mickey Kirkpatrick
Myron Murry
Danny Ornung
Jimmy Theros

The Blue Tones were a road group that appeared in Indianapolis in the early 1960s. The members were exceptional musicians on the nightclub circuit. When the band eventually left Indianapolis, guitarist/singer Jimmy Theros joined another group and made Indianapolis his home.

By/Counts

Group members include:

Mel James
Robbie McVey
Richie Martin
Jim Theros

This band performed on the local nightclub circuit. It featured former Blue Tones singer Jim Theros, and drummer/vocalist Mel James.

BY/COUNTS (1963)
Left to right: Richie Martin, Robbie McVey, Jim Theros and Mel James

The Cavaliers

The Indianapolis-based Cavaliers performed at teen concerts and local nightclubs. They entertained at the Whiteland Barn and the Westlake Beach Club. On the nightclub circuit, they performed in such clubs as the Dan T and Nick & Jerry's. The Cavaliers was Indiana's version of Dean Martin and Jerry Lewis. Their showmanship and harmony earned them great popularity.

THE CAVALIERS (1960)
Larry Allen and Mike Shane

RAY CHURCHMAN

Ray Churchman

Ray Churchman was born in Connersville and moved to Indianapolis when he was fourteen. After taking lessons from drummer Melvin Miller and graduating from Shortridge High School, he joined the Army and performed with the U.S. Army Band until 1945. Ray performed at The Embers, The B&B nightclub and such venues as Clowes Hall and the Fox Burlesque. He backed up artists like Zoot Sims, Pete Fountain, Mel Tormé, Ernie Ford, Wayne Newton and Buddy Greco. In 1958, Churchman was a staff musician for Channel 13 and performed for the *George Willeford Show* and *Don Melvoin Show*. In 1977, Indiana Governor Bowen and Indianapolis Mayor Richard Hudnut honored Churchman for his musical services to the city. Ray was married to the popular television and radio personality Carolyn Churchman, and often performed on her shows. Ray Churchman passed away in September of 2006.

The Classmen

Group members include:

Jim Bruhn
Dick Donahue
Dave Ellman
Mel James

This Indianapolis group was derived from some of Indiana's past bands. Singer Jim Bruhn was a member of The Five Stars, Dick Donahue played with the Dawnbeats and Dave Ellman evolved from Keetie & The Kats. The Classmen were known for their vocal harmony. They also performed comic routines.

THE CLASSMEN

The Crackerjacks

Group members include:

Gary Bedell
Larry Goshen
Paul Hutchinson
Jack Scott
Gene Wittherholt

The Crackerjacks were re-formed from the Indiana touring band The Five Checks. Although most members of the rock group were from Indianapolis, many of their engagements were in Illinois and Missouri. The Crackerjacks disbanded in 1964. Bedell, Goshen, Hutchinson and Scott returned to perform in Indianapolis.

THE CRACKERJACKS
Top row, left to right: Gene Witherholt, Gary Bedell and Jack Scott.
Bottom row: Larry Goshen and Paul Hutchinson.

Bobby Dark

Indianapolis-based singer Bobby Dark was popular in the late 1960s and early 1970s. He performed at some of Indy's top nightspots, including The Hungry I and The Red Frog. Dark occasionally performed with the group Chain Reaction. It featured his sister, Darlene Dowler.

BOBBY DARK
& DARLENE DOWLER

The Dawnbeats (2)

THE DAWNBEATS (2)
Left to right: Tony Nasser, Morgan Schumacher, Larry Lee, Dave Ellman and Larry Gardner

Group members include:
Dave Ellman
Larry "Wazoo" Gardner
Larry Lee
Tony Nasser
Morgan Schumacher

Morgan Schumacher, founding member of the original Dawnbeats, formed this group in 1960. They performed on the nightclub circuit in the Indianapolis area. Saxophonist Tony Nasser lives in Cincinnati and is a regular member of the popular oldies group, Hot Wax. Drummer Morgan Schumacher went on to perform for Haley's Comets, a group derived from music legend Bill Haley's old band.

Del & The Road Runners

DEL & THE ROAD RUNNERS
Left to right: Eddie Green, Delbert Bailey, Dallas Reynolds, Kenny Lee Kernodle and Al Ficklin

Group members include:
Delbert Bailey
Jim Bowers
Ramon Lopez

This country/rock band worked the Indianapolis bar circuit, performing with different members. Later members included Furman Brown, Jerry Collins, Al Ficklin, Eddie Green, Willie Phillips and Dallas Reynolds. Drummer Ramon Lopez played percussion for the Stan Kenton Orchestra.

DEL & THE ROAD RUNNERS (LEFT)
Left to right: Furman Brown, Delbert Bailey, Willie (Phillips) Jones, Jim Bowers (On stage at the Pla-mor Tavern)

DEL & THE ROAD RUNNERS (1961)
Left to right: Delbert Bailey, Ramon Lopez and Jim Bowers

Left to right: Bill Stewart (Crowns) – Delbert Bailey (Road Runners) – Charlie Rich (on stage at the Starlite Paladium)

Duke Demaree

Indianapolis-born Duke Demaree took his first drum lesson at age four from his father John, who was drummer for the famous Charlie Davis Band. Duke played drums during his high school years. After graduating, he continued to pursue music as a career. He performed with many local bands, and in 1962 toured with the group The Pacesetters. This band performed with such artists as Troy Shondell, Rusty Draper, and Little Anthony & The Imperials.

In 1965, Duke joined the group Scarlets, which included Gary Belaire, Dino Patterson, Boyd Rogers, Bunis Rogers and Wes Charles. He later returned to Indianapolis and continued to perform with bands on the local nightclub scene.

THE PACESETTERS (1962)
Left to right: John Ness, Duke Demaree, Danny Ornung, Myron Murry and Larry Dowd (not pictured)

Danny Dollar & The Coins

Group members include:

Tommy Adams
Danny Dollar
Ralph Meyers
Gary McCarty
Don Wilson

This nightclub group featured popular 1950s singer Danny Dollar. The Coins performed at the White Front Tavern and other clubs around the Indianapolis area. Danny (Dowlar) Dollar died August of 2010.

DANNY DOLLAR & THE COINS
Left to right: Don Wilson, Gary McCarty, Danny Dollar, Tommy Adams and Ralph Meyers

The Dominoes

Group members include:

Paul Gray
Harvey Grove
Fred Lawson
Rondo Loschky
Bill Roberts

The Dominoes performed on the Indianapolis bar scene. They backed up many musical acts, including The Monograms.

The Dukes

THE DUKES
Top row, left to right: Jim Hickman, Chuck Best and Dick Walters.
Front row: Jim Sonday.

Group members include:

Gary Bedell
Chuck Best
Jim Hickman
Jim Sonday
Dick Walters

The Dukes, formed in 1961, performed in the Indianapolis area. They began by playing teen dances with DJ Dick Summer. The Dukes became popular during the twist craze era and performed at the Rail Club, an Indianapolis hot spot. At the Rail Club, the Dukes filled the room nightly with a capacity audience. They were so successful that the club changed its name to the Peppermint Lounge. It attracted Chubby Checker and Joey Dee and The Starliters.

After the Dukes left, the club owner obtained rights to the band name, and the band was forced to use The Original Dukes as its new title. The Dukes changed personnel and later included Marden Baker, Gary Bedell, Bob Crabtree, Al Officer and Fred Williams.

Ellman-James Duo

Group members include:

Dave Ellman
Mel James

This duo was formed around 1967. They entertained on the Indianapolis nightclub circuit. Mel James (Melvin Walden-James) later became a jazz journalist and has written for many popular publications.

The Epics

Group members include:

Art Adams
Harvey Grove
Paul Hutchinson
Jack Scott
Gary Thaxton

This group from Indianapolis worked the local bar scene and featured popular rock-a-billy singer Art Adams. The Epics performed in such clubs as The Fortress and the Hungry I. Later members included Bill Stewart and Guy Tarrents.

THE EPICS
Left to right: Paul Hutchinson, Guy Tarrents, Art Adams, Gary Thaxton and Bill Stewart

THE EPICS (1965)
Left to right: Harvey Grove, Paul Hutchinson, Art Adams, Gary Thaxton and Jack Scott

The Five Checks

PHOTO CREDIT: CALE & WHITE

THE FIVE CHECKS (1963)

Top row, left to right: Paul Hutchinson, Delbert Bailey and Bob Edwards. Bottom row: Larry Goshen and Bill Roberts.

Group members include:

Delbert Bailey
Bob Edwards
Larry Goshen
Paul Hutchinson
Bill Roberts

This group, formed in 1963, performed in nightclubs throughout the Midwest. Top vocals and comedy made them popular at such venues as Club Idaho in Terre Haute, The Decatur Lounge in Decatur, Illinois, and Nick & Jerry's in Indianapolis. When members changed, the band became known as The Crackerjacks. Singer Delbert Bailey passed away in January of 2017, and saxophonist Paul Hutchinson died on November 10, 2018.

The Five Chords

THE FIVE CHORDS (1962)

Group members include:

Rod Derks
Harry Kellett
Jack Lewis
Arley Price
Jerry Woodward

This show group from Terre Haute was very popular in the Indianapolis area. They performed at such cubs as the Boom Boom Room and the Pink Poodle. They recorded "Red Wine"/"I Dream of Jeanie" (1960) on the CUCA label, and "I Need Your Loving/Bedelia Brown" (1961) on SOMA. In 1962 they released a live album on the Boom Label titled, *The Five Chords Live at the Boom Boom Room.* Two earlier members of the group were Glenn Pharris and Byron Small.

The First Impression

Group members include:

Dal Baker
Dave Ellman
Melvin (Mel) James

The First Impression, from Indianapolis, included former members from many other groups, including Keetie & The Kats, The Classmen, Ellman-James Duo and the By/Counts. With their refreshing harmonies, The First Impression proved to be very popular on the nightclub scene.

THE FIRST IMPRESSION
Left to right: Dave Ellman, Dal Baker and Melvin (Mel) James

Flo Garvin

Flo Garvin was born in Indianapolis. She was performing at age sixteen on the famous Indiana Avenue. In 1952, Garvin made her first recording on the King label. Her original songs, "I'm On The Outside Looking In" and "Let Me Keep You Warm," featured legendary saxophonist Jimmy Coe. In the late 1950s, she hosted her own television show, *Sentimental Journey*, on station WFBM. In 1999, Flo Garvin was presented The Jazz Hall of Fame Award from the Indianapolis Jazz Foundation.

FLO GARVIN (1960)

SUZANNE PRINCE BAND

Left to right: Steve Kennedy, Suzanne Prince, Debbie Campbell, Gilbert Gordon, Larry Lobdell, Carol McKeeman and Sam Oliver. Recorded one album, "Rusty Nails & Promises."

Gilbert "Gil" Gordon

Gilbert Gordon was born in Indianapolis, and he attended Harry E. Wood High School. Raised in a musical family, Gilbert studied guitar at age twelve and later became an accomplished pianist. He toured with singer Eddie Cash and performed at the Flamingo and MGM Grand Hotel in Las Vegas. In Indianapolis, Gordon has played keyboard with The Suzanne Prince Band, Jimmy Guilford and the Groove Brothers, Tommy Wills, singer Ronnie Haig, and many others.

Jimmy Guilford

JIMMY GUILFORD

Singer Jimmy Guilford started his career at any early age by tap-dancing on street corners for pennies. In the 1950s, he performed with the group the Boppers. Later, he joined the Twilighters, Lamplighters, the Four Sounds and the Monograms. Guilford performed a duo with singer Jimmy Scruggs, and later formed the groups Three Way Street and The Groove Brothers.

In the 1990s, Guilford performed regularly at the American Cabaret Theatre and appeared in the productions of *Summer Lovin'* and *Streetcorner Harmony.* Guilford's recordings include "Misery Street"/"I Want To Be Your Baby" on the Detroit label, Wheelsville, "Too Late To Cry"/"No Body Loves Me" on Thelma Records, and "Heart Breaker"/"I Wanna Be Your Baby" on the Solid Hit label.

Hook, Line and Sinker

Group members include:

Eva Joe
Denver Lee
Tony Little
Danny Stafford

This Indianapolis nightclub act entertained around Indiana from the 1960s through the 1990s.

Inner Circle

Group members include:

Larry Burch
John Hurst
Larry Lee
Guy Tarrents

This band, formed around 1967 and toured throughout the Midwest. Indianapolis native Larry Lee was a former member of Keetie & The Kats.

INNER CIRCLE (1967)

Jess and The Jokers

Group members include:

Bob Brown
Furman Brown
Jess Colburn
Dave Hall
Jerry Hall
Larry Scott
Chuck Wallace
Rex Wamsley

From the Indianapolis area, this band was formed in the early 1960s. The Jokers were mainly a four or five-piece group, but had many member changes. The above is the all-around list of members who made this group popular.

JESS AND THE JOKERS (1961)
Left to right: Larry Scott, Jess Colburn and Rex Wamsley

THE JEWELS (1960)
Live at the Indiana Roof Ballroom

The Jewels

Group members include:

Bill Cooper
Bill Fliehman
Paul Hutchinson
Gary LeMaster

The Jewels were formed in 1959 in Huntington, West Virginia. During a road tour through Indianapolis in 1960, they were booked at the downtown nightclub Nick & Jerry's. After playing that club off and on for a few years, two members of The Jewels made Indianapolis their home. Saxophonist Paul Hutchinson met his wife Darlene at Nick & Jerry's. After his marriage, Paul continued to perform and live in the Indianapolis area. Paul performed with the late Bobby Darrin,

CONTINUED ON PAGE 91

THE JEWELS (1961)
Left to right: Bill Cooper, Bill Fliehman, Paul Hutchinson and Gary LeMaster. On stage at the Stables Nightclub, Anderson, Indiana

The Five Checks, Art Adams and many others. Guitarist/Singer Gary LeMaster, a Coal Grove, Ohio, native, continued to live and perform in the Indianapolis area. Gary joined the popular Indianapolis band Keetie & The Kasuals. Later, he became a member of Bobby Rey's band, The Hollywood Argyles. In 1969, Gary settled in Las Vegas and played various casinos. He became entertainment director for several hotels and casinos. LeMaster performed at the California Hotel, Sams Town and the Stardust. He met his wife Valerie, also a performer, in Las Vegas. In 1986, Gary became a permanent member of the legendary group the Sons of the Pioneers and continued to perform until his passing in September of 2012.

THE SONS OF THE PIONEERS

Left to right: Gary LeMaster is second from left (sitting). Back (middle) Sunny Spencer, original member of the Sons Of The Pioneers.

Jimmy & The Exceptions

Group members include:

Delbert Bailey
Jimmy Bowers
Willie Phillips
Guy Tarrents

This Indianapolis bar band was formed around 1966. It featured popular singers Delbert Bailey and Jimmy Bowers. Other members were Willie Phillips on keyboard; and Guy Tarrents, former drummer of Rooker & The Rockers.

JIMMY & THE EXCEPTIONS

Left to right: Jimmy Bowers, Guy Tarrents, Willie Phillips and Delbert Bailey

Katalinas

Group members include:

Dick Neat
Ronnie Schrock
Gil Work

This group was formed in 1963. They performed on the Indianapolis bar circuit. Later, the band featured popular 1950s teen singer Gary Gillespie.

Keetie & The Kasuals

Group members include:
Dave Kellie
Gary LeMaster
Keith Phillips
Bill Settles
Donny Sanders

Formerly Keetie & The Kats, the group performed on the Indianapolis nightclub scene. They appeared at such clubs as Nick & Jerry's and the Lemon Twist Lounge, and later toured throughout the Midwest. A later member was musician Bob Snyder of Danville, Indiana, who was formerly with the Tommy Dorsey Orchestra. Keith Phillips later purchased a restaurant in California, Gary LeMaster joined the Sons of the Pioneers and Donny Sanders became a popular studio musician in Nashville, recording for Barbara Mandrell and Lee Greenwood.

ORLY KNUTSON TRIO
Left to right: Glen Douglas, Orly Knutson and Jimmy Ganzberg

Orly Knutson Trio

Group members include:

Glen Douglas
Jimmy Ganzberg
Orly Knutson

This trio performed on the Indianapolis nightclub circuit during the late 1960s and early 1970s. The group featured radio personality Orly Knutson, pianist Jimmy Ganzberg, and popular saxophonist Glen Douglas.

Tommy Lam

Indianapolis singer Tommy Lam began performing in the late 1950s and continued through the 1960s and into the 1970s. Tommy fronted his own band through this period. He recorded two singles. "Speed Limit" (1958) on Nabor Records and "Blue Willow" (1959), on the Randall label. The recording of "Speed Limit" has become highly collectible.

TOMMY LAM

Kenny Lee & The Royals

Group members include:

Jerry Collins
Paul Gray
Eddie Green
Kenny Lee Kernodle
Larry Goshen

This group, formed around 1962, performed variety shows and appeared at the popular Boom Boom Room in Indianapolis. The Royals featured singer/guitarist Kenny Lee, saxophonist Jerry Collins, and keyboardist Paul Gray. Drummer Larry Goshen, who replaced Eddie Green, later became a member of the road group The Five Checks.

Jimmy McDaniels

Indianapolis musician Jimmy McDaniels is not only well known for his striking piano arrangements and his stylish vocals, but he's also an accomplished saxophonist.

Jimmy performed and conducted for such artists as June Christy, Nat "King" Cole, Rosemary Clooney and Mel Tormé. He also hosted a radio show on station WSMJ for two years. In 1969, Jimmy recorded for the JMCA label a self-title album *Jimmy McDaniels*. Jimmy passed away on April 25, 2009.

PHOTO CREDIT: LARRY GOSHEN

Left to right: Jimmy McDaniels and Pete Funk. Jam Session (1963)

The Monograms

Group members include:

Charlie Anderson
Bob Bernard
Bob "Chico" Penick
John Vardiman

The Monograms were formed in 1959 in Indianapolis. The combination of friendship and showmanship made this an unforgettable group. The Monograms performed in such clubs as Nick & Jerry's, Minardo's, Starlite Paladium, the Mad Pad, Rail Club and the Hungry I. Their last performance was June 14, 1986 at Indy's Heart of Rock n' Roll Reunion. Even though Charlie Anderson was ill, they gave a fantastic performance. Charlie passed away just a few months later. Two other members that performed with the group were George Black and Jimmy Guilford.

THE MONOGRAMS
Top to bottom: Bob Bernard, Bob (Chico) Penick, John Vardiman and George Black

THE MONOGRAMS (1963)
Top to bottom: Charlie Anderson, Bob Bernard, Bob (Chico) Penick and John Vardiman

Mary Moss

Mary Moss was born in Louisville, Kentucky. She moved to Indianapolis in 1958. Her first local engagement occurred at the Thunderbird Nightclub in Fountain Square with recording artist Boyd Bennett. Moss later performed at The Embers, the B&B Lounge, the Pink Poodle and LaRue's Supper Club. In the 1960s, she performed in Chicago at the Playboy Club, and continued to work the popular Playboy circuit. She also performed as half of the 1950s and '60s nightclub duo King and Mary. Mary continued to perform at the Jazz Kitchen, Jazz Fest and other venues. She also produced several variety shows at the Walker Theatre titled *Les Beaux Art au Feminin!* This show featured all-female entertainers and was subtitled *Women Simply Kickin' It!* Mary Moss passed away on January 8, 2016.

MARY MOSS

KING AND MARY

The Original Dukes

THE ORIGINAL DUKES (1964)
Left to right: Richie Martin, Chuck Best, Jim Sonday and Jim Hickman

Group members include:

Chuck Best
Jim Hickman
Richie Martin
Jim Sonday

This group was formed in the mid-1960s. They were former members of the Dukes. Forced to change their name due to a nightclub conflict (See Dukes, this section) this band continued to perform at the Lemon Twist and other local clubs. They recorded one forty-five "Ain't About To Lose My Cool" and "It Looks Like Rain" on Down Home Records. Other members included Dick Walters and Fred Williams.

THE ORIGINAL DUKES
Left to right: Fred Williams, Jim Hickman and Dick Walters

The Keith Phillips VI

THE KEITH PHILLIPS VI

Group members include:

Pete Duquesne
Dave Kellie
Keith Phillips
Bill Settles
Skip Wagner
Bruce Waterman

This band was formed in the mid-1960s. It was the last of the Keetie & the Kats clan. Three members of this group, Dave Kellie, Keith Phillips and Bill Settles, were from the Indianapolis area. The Keith Phillips VI performed at Al Hirt's Club in New Orleans, the Beachcomber in Boston and the Sheraton in Puerto Rico. They appeared on national television with such artists as Al Hirt and Mike Douglas.

Salt & Pepper

SALT & PEPPER (1969)
Bill Bogby and Dan Hailey

Group members include:

Bill Bogby
Dan Hailey

The original Salt & Pepper was formed around 1962. It consisted of Bill Bogby and Bill Lynch. In the 1960s, Dan Hailey (formerly with the Outsiders) joined Bogby to form the new Salt & Pepper. This popular duo performed in Indianapolis at such clubs as the Holyoke and the Hungry I.

Screaming Jimmy

Screaming Jimmy (James Churchwell) was a popular soul singer in the Indianapolis area in the early 1960s. He performed at local nightclubs and was an occasional singer with Del & The Road Runners. This band performed regularly at the Fountain Square in Indianapolis.

SCREAMING JIMMY (1963)
Left to right: Ramon Lopez, Screaming Jimmy (Jimmy Churchwell), Delbert Bailey and Jim Bowers

THE SPORTSMEN (1964)
Left to right: Bill Roberts, Larry Goshen, John Scott and Rondo Loschky

The Sportsmen

Group members include:

Rondo Loschky
Larry Goshen
Bill Roberts
John Scott

The Sportsmen was a top-forty band from Indianapolis that worked the local bar scene. Formed in 1964, they played the popular go-go clubs and performed in such places as the Madison Lounge, Rat Fink Room, Hungry I and the Stardust Show Lounge. This group was together through the 1960s and disbanded around 1970.

The Swingin' Lads

Group members include:

Jim Bruhn
Ron Carroll
Jim Carsey
Don Kelley
Bill Lynch
Manny Paris

The Swingin' Lads consisted of Don Kelley, former member of Terre Haute's popular teen group The Fascinators, and Jim Bruhn, former member of the Indianapolis group The Five Stars. Other members included Ron Carroll, Bill Lynch and Manny Paris.

This fantastic show group attracted substantial attention by using powerful dance routines, smooth vocals, and exciting instrumentals. Touring as one of the top entertaining acts in the United States, they performed at show clubs in Las Vegas, Reno and Lake Tahoe. They appeared with such artists as Louis Armstrong, Judy Garland, Tom Jones and the Nicholas Brothers, to name a few. Television appearances include the *Dean Martin Show* and the *Ed Sullivan Show* (six times).

THE SWINGIN' LADS

Manny Paris, in front, with (left to right) Jim Bruhn, Ron Carroll and Don Kelley standing behind him. Photographed with Las Vegas showgirls, including actress Goldie Hawn on Bill Lynch's left.

THE SWINGIN' LADS

Left to right: actor Frank Gorshin, Ron Carroll, Manny Paris, Don Kelley and Jim Dale (Bruhn)

THE SWINGIN' LADS

Photo on left: left to right: Ron Carroll, Don Kelley, Ed Sullivan and Jim Dale (Bruhn)

Center photo: left to right: Ron Carroll, Tom Jones, Don Kelley and Jimmy Dale (Bruhn)

Left photo, left to right: Don Kelley, Louis Armstrong and Ron Carroll

THE SWINGIN' LADS (1966)

Front row, left to right: Manny Paris, Don Kelley and Jim Bruhn. Back row, left to right: Bill Lynch and Ron Carroll.

TEACH & THE TRACERS (1969)
Left to right: Morgan Schumacher, Jimmy Theros and Larry Gardner, with Teach Theros in front.

Teach & The Tracers

Group members include:

Larry "Wazoo" Gardner
Morgan "Furgie" Schumacher
Jimmy Theros
Teach Theros

This Indianapolis bar band performed in the late 1960s. It featured husband/wife duo Jimmy and Teach Theros, ex-Downbeats drummer Morgan Schumacher, and ex-Keetie & The Kats bass player, Wazoo.

THE TRAVELLS (1968)
Left to right: Kenneth Smith, Eugene Smith andEddie "Little Eddie" Jeffers, with Jackie Asher in front.

The Travells

Group members include:

Jackie Asher (Jacobsen)
Eddie "Little Eddie" Jeffers
Eugene Smith
Kenneth Smith

This band from Indianapolis was fronted by singer/ guitarist Eugene Smith. The Travells were a long-lasting group that changed members like the change of seasons. Other members include Gary Hamilton, Paul Jackson, Gary Jacobsen, Dave Jones, Ronald Khert, and Tom Spencer.

Tuttle & The Shells

Group members include:

Glen Douglas
Jimmy Ganzberg
Gary McKiernan
Mike Tuttle

This quartet from Indianapolis performed a mixture of pop and jazz. The Shells included saxophonist Glen Douglas and popular keyboardist Jimmy Ganzberg. They played the local club circuit and performed a long engagement at the West Sixteenth Street pub Whitefront.

TUTTLE & THE SHELLS
Left to right: Jimmy Ganzberg, Mike Tuttle, Glen Douglas and Gary McKiernan

Eddie Walker & The Demons

Group members include:

George Able
Larry (Wazoo) Gardner
Gene Robinson
Morgan Schumacher
Eddie Walker

The Demons from Indianapolis performed in the local night-club circuit. Featured singer Eddie Walker recorded two singles, "Twistin' Your Life Away" (1963) on the Keet label, and "I Don't Need You Anymore" on Mew Records.

EDDIE WALKER & THE DEMONS (1963)
Left to right: Gene Robinson, George Able, Eddie Walker, Larry Gardner and Morgan "Furgie" Schumacher

Step Wharton

STEP WHARTON

Step Wharton was a popular lounge pianist/singer who performed in the Indianapolis area in the 1950s and '60s. One of his most popular engagements was at downtown night-spot the Sherwood Pub.

Dean Wolfe

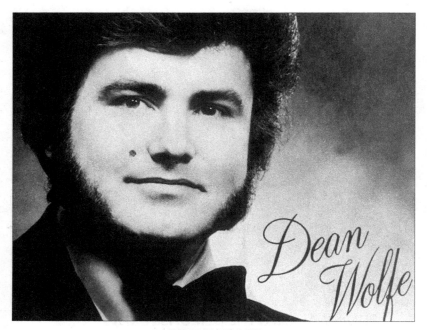

DEAN WOLFE

Bands included:

Dean Wolfe & The Wolfe Pack
Dean Wolfe & The Red Men
Dean Wolfe & The Second Chapter

Dean Wolfe performed in the Indianapolis area through the 1960s. Even though the bands had many sub-titles, the name Dean Wolfe will always be remembered on the local nightclub circuit.

The
Swell
Seventies

The Swell Seventies

The era of the 1970s began as America bombed Vietcong supply routes in Cambodia. The war spread to Laos, with no end in sight. The U.S. punished one of its own when Lt. William Calley was convicted of premeditated murder for his actions at the My Lai Massacre.

In 1972, Richard M. Nixon was inaugurated as President. Watergate proved his downfall and he resigned. Vice-President, Spiro Agnew was disgraced as well. In 1976, Jimmy Carter and Gerald Ford debated the fate of America. The voters chose the Georgia governor to lead the nation.

By 1972, *Fiddler On The Roof* became the longest running Broadway show in history. In 1973, Indiana-born Kurt Vonnegut, Jr. wrote his finest novel, *Breakfast of Champions.*

Francis Ford Coppola added his version of the history of the Mafia with the Godfather classics. In 1977, the world mourned the loss of singer Bing Crosby.

As the nation coped with the Vietnam War, music during the 1970s reflected a country searching for an identity. Perhaps the R&B song by Timmy Thomas, "Why Can't We Live Together?" was symbolic of the attitude.

Burt Bacharach began the decade with the hit tune, "Raindrops Keep Falling On My Head," from the film *Butch Cassidy and the Sundance Kid,* starring Paul Newman and Robert Redford. Other songs of note included "Maggie May" by Rod Stewart, the Rolling Stones' "Brown Sugar," "My Sweet

Lord," "A Horse With No Name," and "Me and Bobby McGee."

Indiana's version of '70s music produced a plethora of stars. They included The Faith Band, John Hiatt, Jubal, Roadmaster, David Lee Roth of Van Halen, and John "Cougar" Mellencamp. As the decade roared to a close, Disco became the fad, as John Travolta lit up the screen in *Saturday Night Fever*. Clubs across Indiana began to play the upbeat music to the delight of fans.

Soul music also flourished in Indiana. Groups such as Black Magic, Fresh, and Manchild were popular. A young kid from Gary, Indiana began to work his way into the headlines as well. His name was Michael Jackson.

Indiana in the late '60s and early '70s produced an abundance of R&B, soul and funk entertainers and record labels. Herb Miller's Lamp Records was one, they debut their first release of "Somebody Please" by the Vanguards. Other Indiana groups and labels were James Bell & The Highlighters, RoJam, Little Murry & The Mantics on 700 West, Allison & Calvin Turner, LuLu and The Rhythem Machine on Rodan. Locals like Rodney Stepp of The Diplamatics, bassist Larry King and keyboardist Allen "Turk" Burke went on to perform in the touring back-up band for the Spinners and Marvin Gaye. Other Indiana soul groups remembered were The Moonlighters, The Pearls, Revolution, Compared to What, Words of Wisdom and The Ebony Rhythm Funk Campaign. Just to name a few.

Others that made their mark during *The Swell Seventies* include:

THE AMERICAN CAST (1971)

The American Cast

Group members include:

Keith Dollins
Dan Hall
Pat McArdle
Scott McDowell
Jeff Roy
Scott Wallace

Popular in the 1970s, this Indianapolis band originated at North Central High School. Originally called the Screamin' A's, they later became The American Cast.

AMNESTY

Left to right: Kirk Alexander, James Massie, Calvin Williams, Joe Trotter, Damon Malone, Rafael Barnes and Geno Johnson, with Herman Walker in front.

Amnesty

Group members include:

Kirk Alexander
Rafael Barnes
Geno Johnson
Damon Malone
James Massie
Joe Trotter
Herman Walker
Calvin Williams

This Indianapolis R&B soul group was formed around 1968. They performed on stage with The Jackson 5, The O'Jays, Kool & The Gang and many others. Their 1970s recordings include "Lord Help Me"/"Three Cheers For My Baby" on Two West Records, and "Everybody Who Wants To Be Free" on the Lamp label.

Black Magic

Group members include:

Allen "Turk" Burke
Duane "Buzzard" Garvin
Joe Jackson
Doby London

BLACK MAGIC (1973)
Left to right: Doby London, Allen "Turk" Burke and Joe Jackson

Formed in 1973, this Indianapolis quartet became a trio after original drummer Duane Garvin departed. Black Magic began playing in Indianapolis clubs such as the End Zone and later performed with many national acts. The group featured keyboardist Allen "Turk" Burke, who was born and raised in Indianapolis. Burke attended Shortridge High School and began playing professionally when he was around sixteen. He continued to perform with such artists as Patti LaBelle & The Blue Bells, and the Spinners. That gig provided the opportunity for him to become music arranger and a permanent band member of The Spinners. In 1974, Allen toured with the famous Marvin Gaye. He later moved back to Indiana to join the local group Fresh. He then formed the group Fingers. He continues to perform in the Indianapolis area.

The Champion Band

Group members include:

Bruce "Snooky" Coons
Bob Jones
Charlie "Chuck" Kendal
David "Beaugie" Wait
Loren "Lo" Woods

This rock group from Indianapolis was formed around 1975. Original members were Jason Becket, David Miller and former Roadmaster musician Adam Smasher (Asher Benruby). Around 1976, Adam Smasher and David Miller left the group and were replaced by the members listed at left. In the 1980s, Adam Smasher became a popular DJ, and Loren "Lo" Woods performed with the band Jubal. In 1991, Woods recorded a solo album titled *It Might Take Years.*

Darlene Dollar (Dowler)

(Darlene Early)

An Indianapolis native, Darlene Dollar began her singing career when she was fourteen. She performed at local teen clubs and record hops in the early 1960s. In the 1970s, she toured the local nightclub circuit. Darlene was the vocalist with her brother's band, Bobby Dark and The Chain Reaction, and later performed with the group Sunshine Way. After moving to Daytona Beach, Darlene joined the group Tyme. She is now retired from the music business.

DARLENE DOWLER WITH SUNSHINE WAY
(1970)

THE CHAIN REACTION (1972)
Front row, left to right: Bobby Dark, Darlene Dowler and Gary Thaxton. Back row, left to right: Doug Sterns, Paul Gray, John Scott, (unidentified), Ron Schrock and Gil Work.

The Faith Band

Group members include:

Dave Barnes
Dave Bennett
John Cascella
Mark Cawley
Carl Storie

THE FAITH BAND (1978)
Left to right: Carl Storie, John Cascella (keyboards), Dave Barnes (drums), Mark Cawley (bass) and Dave Bennett (guitar)

The Faith Band may be the longest running band to emerge from the Indianapolis area. Formed as The Chosen Few in 1967, they evolved into the group Limousine five years later. In 1973, they changed their name to The Faith Band. They recorded "Dancin' Shoes" in 1978. It reached #54 on the Billboard charts. In 1979, they peaked at the #76 position with "You're My Weakness." Both were recorded on the Mercury label. One member, Carl Storie, continues to entertain in the Indianapolis area. In the 1990s, he performed with the Alligator Brothers and later produced and recorded his own CD. Band member John Cascella recorded and toured with the John Mellencamp band. He died of a heart attach on November 14, 1992. The Faith Band recordings include *Faith* 1973, United Artists Records, *Excuse Me…I Just Cut An Album* (1977), Village Records. And *Rock 'n Romance* (1978), *Face To Face* (1979) and *Vital Signs* (1979) were all recorded on the Village/Phonogram label.

The Fifth Amendment

Group members include:

Larry Goshen
Paul Gray
Louie McCane
Tom Rodgers
John Scott

THE FIFTH AMENDMENT (1975)
Front row, left to right: Louie McCane and Larry Goshen. Back row, left to right (back): John Scott, Tom Rodgers and Paul Gray.

Formed in 1975, this Indianapolis band performed top forty cover tunes on the Indiana nightclub circuit. Later, saxophonist John Scott joined the Witness band and bassist Tom Rodgers became an Indianapolis policeman.

Richard "Rick" Finch

(K.C. & the Sunshine Band)

Richard Finch was born January 23, 1954 in Indianapolis. Finch played bass guitar and was an important member of the national recording group K.C. & The Sunshine Band. He co-wrote some of their biggest hits, including "Shake Your Booty" and "Get Down Tonight," which in 1975 became number-one on the Billboard charts. Another Sunshine hit penned by Richard and KC (Harry Wayne Casey) was "That's The Way I Like It." Richard also co-wrote "Rock Your Baby" for singer George McCrae. In 1974, that song became number-one on the Billboard charts in both the United States and the United Kingdom.

Fingers

FINGERS
Clockwise from top: Russell Taylor, Allen "Turk" Burke and Bob Schuster

Group members include:
Allen "Turk" Burke
Bob Schuster
Russell Taylor

Formed in the late 1970s, this popular Indiana group was comprised of three talented musicians, Allen "Turk" Burke from Indianapolis, Bob Schuster from Evansville, and Russell Taylor from Anderson. Bob Schuster started his musical career by playing the French horn and studying classical music at Ball State University. Russell Taylor was singing professionally at the age of sixteen. Two years later he became a percussionist. In 1976, he signed with United Artists, and recorded one album with the Peddler Band titled *Street Corner Stuff*. The Fingers trio performed in some of the most popular nightclubs in Indianapolis and also toured the United States. They performed locally at clubs such as Pierpont's, the Hilton and the popular Glass Parrot. (For information on Allen "Turk" Burke, refer to the groups Fresh and Magic in this section.)

Five Easy Pieces

Group members include:

Chuck Cunningham
Charlie Hinkle
Bonnie McDowell
Robin McDowell
Les Szigethy

Formed in 1972, Five Easy Pieces performed on the Indiana nightclub circuit. They entertained at such clubs as The Garage in Broad Ripple, and Steckleys in Carmel. This group has opened for such acts as Three Dog Night, The Lettermen and comedian Rich Little. They also recorded a vinyl EP that included later members Linda Williams, Sam Leseman and Ron Robbins.

FIVE EASY PIECES (1973)
Left to right: Chuck Cunningham, Bonnie McDowell, Charlie Hinkle, Robin McDowell and Les Szigethy

FIVE EASY PIECES
(RAM-A-LAM & THE DING DONGS)

Fresh

FRESH (1976)

Left to right: Doby London, Kathy Strakis, Bill Lancton, Ray Petronzio and Allen "Turk" Burke

Group members include:

Allen "Turk" Burke
Bill Lancton
Doby London
Ray Petronzio
Kathy Strakis

Fresh was formed in Indianapolis in 1974. It was one of the most popular funk and R&B bands to play in the area. The group performed at top Indiana nightclubs such as the Sheraton East, the Enterprise and the Vogue. They toured extensively in over twenty states. Keyboardist Allen "Turk" Burke performed with many major stars such as Marvin Gaye, the Spinners and Patti LaBelle. Bill Lancton performed with the popular Indianapolis band Dog Talk, and has recorded two CDs under his own name, *Lanctones* (1995) and *Yeah, Man* (1999). Fresh recorded one album in the 1970s, but it was never released. Other members of Fresh were Rob McCoy, Bill Knipe, Don Davidson, Russell Taylor and Bob Schuster. Fresh disbanded in 1978.

Jack Gilfoy

JIM GERARD AND JACK GILFOY

Live on WFBM-TV (1968)

Indianapolis-born Jack Gilfoy began playing drums at the age of ten. He studied percussion at Indiana University and then continued studies with jazz drummers Shelly Manne, Joe Morello and Peter Erskine. Gilfoy performed with such artists as Sonny & Cher, Ben E. King, Johnny Mathis, the Marvelettes, and the Spinners. In 1965, Gilfoy opened a recording studio in Bloomington. He recorded Roadmaster, the Wright Brothers Overland Stage, and John Mellencamp's first album, *Chestnut Street Incident.* For thirty years, Gilfoy was drummer for the Henry Mancini Orchestra. In 1971, he toured for a short time with the king himself, Elvis Presley. Jack Gilfoy passed away on May 3, 2008.

Gizmos

Group members include:

Tim Carroll
Steve Feikes
Phil Hundley
Dale Lawrence
Shadow Myers
Ted Niemiec
Billy Nightshade
Robbie Wise

The Indiana-based Gizmos, composed of different members, performed together from 1975 through 1981. Recordings produced in the 1970s were recently re-released on Gulcher, an underground record label originally based in Bloomington. John Mellencamp appeared briefly on one of their recordings, "Boring, Part 1," performing back-up guitar and vocals.

Good Seed

Group members include:

Doug Adams
Greg Anderson
Chris Browning
Rich Gootee
Billy Warren

This group from Indiana was formed in the mid-1970s. They recorded two albums, *Rooted & Grounded* (1974), and self-titled *Good Seed* (1976), on Village Records.

Jimmy Guilford Band (Three Way Street)

Group members include:

Erroll Grandy
Jimmy Guilford
Mingo Jones
Danny Smith

This band performed on the Indianapolis nightclub circuit. Organist Erroll Grandy and bassist Mingo Jones were popular players on the jazz circuit. Jones continued to perform in the Indianapolis area. Grandy died in June of 1991. Guilford was a regular cast member of the American Cabaret Theatre.

JIMMY GUILFORD BAND (1978)
Left to right: Mingo Jones, Jimmy Guilford, Erroll Grandy and Danny Smith

John Hiatt

John Hiatt was born in Indianapolis on August 20, 1952. Influenced by black artists such as the Isley Brothers and Otis Redding, he purchased a guitar at a young age and taught himself how to play. Two of the early bands John joined were, The Four Fifth and Joe Lynch and The Hangmen. In the early 1970s, Hiatt moved to Nashville and began his songwriting career for the famous Tree Publishing House. Country singer Tracey Nelson recorded several of his songs. John Hiatt recorded his own songs on his first album titled, *Hanging 'Round The Observatory* (1974). He released records on Epic, MCA, Geffen, A&M, and Capitol. Hiatt records for the Vanguard label, and his first release "Crossing Muddy Waters," (1999) was nominated for a Grammy Award in the Best Traditional Blues Album category.

Hyjinks (Empire)

Group members include:

Albert Bearman
John Dinwiddie
Dallas Miller
Al Roth

This Indiana band was formed in the late 1970s. After the replacement of bassist Dallas Miller with Jayson Jones, Hyjinks became Empire. This group was successful in the Indianapolis area. A recording was released on the 2nd *Home Grown* album. Later they became the opening band for John "Cougar" Mellencamp at Market Square Arena in Indianapolis.

Jermaine Jackson

Jermaine Jackson was born in Gary in 1954. He was an original member of the Jackson Family Singers before joining the Jackson 5 singing group in 1964. After a successful tour with The Jacksons, Jermaine recorded his first solo album in 1972. It was titled simply, *Jermaine.* His 45-single debut, "That's How Love Goes" climbed to the #46 spot on the Billboard charts. In 1973, he recorded "Daddy's Home," which hit the top 10, earning Jermaine a gold record. He recorded many other albums and singles in the 1980s, earning a fine reputation as a solo artist. He continues to perform for The Jacksons as a soloist. In September 2001, Jermaine joined his brothers, including Michael, for a 20-year reunion concert at New York's Madison Square Garden.

JOHN HIATT

Michael Jackson

MICHAEL JACKSON

Michael Jackson was born on August 29, 1958 in Gary. He began performing at age five. In 1964, Michael joined his brothers to form The Jackson 5. In 1971, Michael began his solo career for Motown Records. "Got To Be There" hit the charts, and propelled him to stardom. Michael recorded many songs in the 1970s, but in 1982, under the direction of producer Quincy Jones, *Thriller* was released. It sold over 40 million copies worldwide and became #1 in the United States and the United Kingdom. The recording received 12 Grammy nominations. It also produced a run of successful hit singles, each accompanied by a promotional video that widened the scope of the genre. To celebrate his 30-year career, CBS television produced a two-day concert at Madison Square Garden in New York. The event was held September 7 and 10, 2001, and included a performance with Britney Spears and a 20-year reunion of The Jackson 5. Michael Jackson died on June 25, 2009.

Jubal

JUBAL (1975)

Front row, left to right: Steve Newbold, Nancy Dorsey and Dave Zerfas. Back row, left to right: Larry McCullough, Bryan Zerfas and Howard Phillips.

Group members include:

Nancy Dorsey
Larry McCullough
Steve Newbold
Howard Phillips
Bryan Zerfas
Dave Zerfas

Jubal, a popular band from Indianapolis, was formed in 1964. Later members include Mark Burton, Jeff Gardner, Chick McHenry, Charlie Smith, Pat Smith and John Smith.

Khazad Doom

Group members include:

Jack Eadon
Steve "Crow" Hilkin
Tom Sievers
Al Yates

This Gary, Indiana, band recorded one album in 1970 titled, *Level 6 1/2* on the LPL label.

The Late Show

Group members include:

Rick Clayton
Don Main
Mark Moran
Chris Pyle

This group from Indianapolis was formed in the late 1970s. They recorded one album in 1980 titled, *Portable Pop*. It was recorded on the Rave label. The group appeared around the Midwest and opened for many top name acts, including The Pretenders, Dr. Hook and Huey Lewis and the News. In the 1980s, they changed their name to Recordio.

Brad Long

Logansport-native Brad Long was born in 1954. He began his music career in 1967 as a percussionist. Long then studied guitar and later became successful on the bass and keyboards. He began playing with the group Celebrate in 1971, and in 1973 joined the band Tobias. He later performed as a single act. In 1978, he recorded "Love Me Again"/"Come To Me" on the Music Stand label. In 1981, Long recorded for the compilation album, *Battle of the Garages*. Brad Long continues to perform special concerts in the Logansport area.

BRAD LONG (1978)

Madison Zane

MADISON ZANE (1976)

Front row, left to right, Don Ewigleben and Paula Bargé. Back row, left to right: Steve Drybread, Jim Benge, Larry Sauer and Joe Stout.

Group members include:

Paula Bargé
Jim Benge
Steve Drybread
Don Ewigleben
Larry Sauer
Joe Stout

This lounge band from Indianapolis was formed in 1976. They recorded one single.

Manchild

MANCHILD (1977)

Group members include:

Chuck Bush
Kenny Edmonds
Reggie Griffin
Robert Parson
Daryl Simmons

The band Manchild was formed in Indianapolis. They recorded for the Chi-Sound label around 1977. Later, singer Kenny Edmonds joined his brothers Kevon and Melvin in their group After 7. Kenny later became known as Babyface, producing artists such as Toni Braxton, Boyz II Men, and Madonna. (Above photo — Kenny Edmonds, back row, third from left.)

Donald McPherson

Indianapolis-born Donald McPherson was an important member of the popular group, The Main Ingredient. They were very successful in 1970 with their hit recording of "I'm So Proud" for RCA Records. The Main Ingredient was originally called, "The Poets." They had recorded "Merry Christmas Baby" on the Red Bird label in 1965. In 1971, Donald McPherson died of leukemia. His replacement in The Main Ingredient was none other than singer Cuba Gooding, father of Academy Award nominated actor, Cuba Gooding Jr.

John "Cougar" Mellencamp

John Mellencamp was born on October 7, 1951 in Seymour. He began his musical career by entertaining in high school. Mellencamp played with the band Crepe Soul for 18 months before being kicked out for his inability to sing well. He joined Snakepit Banana Barn, and after graduating from high school formed the group Trash, which included guitarist Larry Crane. Mellencamp later enjoyed great success by recording under the name of John Cougar. Two popular hits were, "Hurts So Good" and "Jack and Diane."

In 1983, Mellencamp released his first album under the name of John Mellencamp, and his recordings continued to climb the charts. Mellencamp recorded eleven albums from 1976 through 1989 for the Riva label and then Mercury and MCA. In 1992 he starred in and performed the soundtrack for the movie *Falling From Grace*.

Various Indiana members of his past recording sessions include Kenny Aronoff, John Cascella, Dane Clark, Larry Crane, Liza Germano, Dave Grissom, Toby Myers and Mike Wanchic. As a Grammy Winner and member of the Rock N' Roll Hall of Fame, Mellencamp released his latest album in 2018, *Sad Clowns & Hillbillies*.

JOHN MELLENCAMP

Melting Pot

Group members include:

Dick Gentile

Paul Hmurovich

Howie McGurty

Steve Nichols

Joe Rudd

Mickey Smith

Jerry Thompson

Kenny Tibbets

Bill Witherspoon

Consisting of musicians from Indianapolis and other surrounding states, Melting Pot was a great soul group. The group, popular from 1970, was heavy with brass. They recorded one album, *Fire Burn, Cauldron Bubble* (1971), on the Ampex Records label. This album was dedicated to Mickey Smith, who died after a drowning accident.

Omega

Group members include:

Jim Haganman

Al Roth

Monte Stultz

Bruce Wiengart

Four Southport High School students in Indianapolis formed Omega in 1972. This group played locally at the Sherwood and other teen clubs.

Rapture

RAPTURE

Left to right: Herman Walker, Rodney Stepp, Greg Russell, Pheldon J. Majors, Harry Eaton, Lonnie Williams, Tony Hayes and Rodney Borhie

Group members include:

Rodney Borhic

Harry Eaton

Tony Hayes

Pheldon J. Majors

Greg Russell

Rodney Stepp

Herman Walker

Lonnie Williams

R&B soul group Rapture was formed in the late 1970s in Indianapolis. The popular group toured the United States and opened for many big name acts. Member Rodney Stepp became one of the musical directors of the Spinners and continues to perform in the Indianapolis area.

Rich Kids

Group members include:

Dean Childress
Jim Gardner
Jeff Holt
Dave Washburn
Corky Whiteman

RICH KIDS (1976)
Left to right: Jim Gardner, Dave Washburn, Dean Childress, Corky Whiteman and Jeff Holt

This Fowler, Indiana, group recorded three singles, "Dance Your Way into My Heart"/"Always On The Run" (1977), "Oh The Girls"/"Young Kingdom" and "You Always Hurt The One You Love"/"Mars Needs Women," both in 1979.

Roadmaster

Group members include:

Rick Benick
Bobby Johns
Stephen McNally
Toby Myers
Michael Reed
Stephen Riley
Adam Smasher

ROADMASTER

This Indianapolis-based band was discovered at a local nightclub in 1975 by recording artist Todd Rundgren. Roadmaster traveled nationally, and opened for artists such as Ted Nugent, Blue Oyster Cult and Rush. Their first album, *Roadmaster* (1976), was recorded for the Village label. Later they were signed by Mercury, and recorded *Sweet Music* (1978), *Hey World* (1979) and *Fortress* (1980). Adam Smasher, one of the original members who recorded only on the first album, later became a popular Indianapolis disc jockey.

Bass player Toby Myers joined John Mellencamp's band and can be heard on some of his early recordings. Guitarist Rick Benick passed away on June 14, 2018.

David Lee Roth

Born October 10, 1955, in Bloomington, David Lee Roth performed with the Redball Jet band before he was hired to join the popular group Van Halen. Roth's good looks and flamboyant antics and guitarist Eddie Van Halen's talent made Van Halen one of the most popular bands in the 1970s and '80s. This fame occurred after the band played the bar circuit around Pasadena/Santa Barbara for three years. They first became successful with their self-titled album in 1978. It hit number 19 on the charts and eventually sold over six million copies. After many successful recordings, Roth became a solo artist in 1985 and released a four-song EP, *Crazy From The Heat*. It spun off two hit singles, "California Girls," and the Louis Prima song, "Just A Gigolo"/"Ain't Got Nobody."

Screamin' Gypsy Bandits

Group members include:

Bruce Anderson
Mark Bingham
Tina Lane
Bob Lucas
Dale Sophiea

This Bloomington band recorded two LPs, *In The Eye* (1973) and *Dancer Inside You* (1974), both on the BRBQ label. Two members of this band, Bruce Anderson and Dale Sophiea formed the popular San Francisco group, MX 80.

Shiloh Morning

Group members include:

Mark Bouse
Mark Hancock
John McDowell
Jeannie McGill
Ken Scheidler

Formed in the mid-1970s, this band played the Indianapolis nightclub circuit. They recorded one album, the self-titled *Shiloh Morning* (1974).

Them Changes

Group members include:

Bill Dickie
Paul Gray
Ben Hickman
Larry Goshen

This band was formed in 1978. It played the Indianapolis nightclub circuit when disco was at its peak.

THEM CHANGES (1978)
Left to right: Ben Hickman, Larry Goshen, Paul Gray and Bill Dickie

Timmy Thomas

Timmy Thomas was born in Evansville on November 13, 1944. An accomplished singer, songwriter and keyboardist, Thomas performed with jazz icons such as Donald Byrd and Cannonball Adderley. After performing session work with the Memphis-based Goldwax label, he embarked on a solo career. In 1972, Timmy Thomas' Polydor recording of "Why Can't We Live Together" hit #3 on the Billboard charts. He later continued a run of minor R&B hits recorded on Glades Records.

Tobias

Group members include:

Pat Hagene
Steve Kinder
Brad Long
Ted Pitman

Formed in 1973, this band was from the Logansport area. They performed at teen dances and high school events around northern Indiana.

Duke Tumatoe and The All-Star Frogs
Duke Tumatoe and The Power Trio

DUKE TUMATOE & THE ALL-STAR FROGS (1975)
Left to right: Doctor Seuss, Gary Brewer, L.V. Hammond,
Duke Tumatoe and James Hill

Group members include:

Gary Brewer
L.V. Hammond
James Hill
Doctor Seuss
Robin Steele
Duke Tumatoe

Duke Tumatoe and The All-Star Frogs was formed in the 1970s and performed well into the late 1980s. Duke recorded several albums, *Naughty Child* (1981), *Duke Tumatoe And The All Star Frogs* (1982), and *Dukes Up* (1984) on the Blind Pig label. Under the Power Trio name, they recorded *I Like My Job* (1988) on Warner.

Deniece Williams

Soul singer Deniece Williams was born Deniece Chandler on June 3, 1951 in Gary. She recorded her first single in the late 1960s for the Chicago based label Toddlin' Town Records. Williams was hired by Stevie Wonder to join his vocal back-up group and contributed to four of his albums.

After leaving Wonder for a solo career, she recorded her first album, *This is Niecy* (1976) on Columbia. Williams recorded *Songbird* (1977) and then teamed with Johnny Mathis for the big hits, "Too Much Too Little Too Late" and "That's What Friends Are For" (1978).

Williams recorded many songs but became well known for "Let's Hear It For The Boy" (Columbia 1984) from the soundtrack of *Footloose*.

A very successful songwriter, she has penned tunes for such artists as Frankie Valli, The Whispers, Stanley Turrentine, Nancy Wilson and many others.

In the late 1980s, Williams recorded several gospel albums on the Sparrow label, and *This Is My Song* (1998) on Harmony. Her later recordings were not as successful, but she still remains popular with the R&B audience.

Bill Wilson

Bill Wilson was a singer-songwriter from the Indianapolis area. He recorded several albums, including *Every Changing Minstrel* (1973) on the Columbia label, *Talking To Stars* (1976) Bar-Bq Records and *Made In The USA* (1980).

The Wright Brothers

Group members include:

Karl Hinkle
Tim Wright
Tom Wright

Tim and Tom Wright were born in French Lick, Indiana. They first formed the Overland Stage band around 1971, and recorded on their own label, Wright & Perry Records. Around 1980, Karl Hinkle joined the brothers and they became The Wright Brothers band. They recorded for Warner Bros. Records and then the Mercury label.

The Wright Brothers perform a variety of music, including Rock & Roll, Country, Bluegrass and Gospel. They have appeared at the Grand Ole Opry and made special appearances with such entertainers as Bob Hope, Dolly Parton, Ronnie Milsap, and the Coasters, to name a few.

The Wright Brothers also appeared on several television shows such as *Hee Haw*, the *Ralph Emery Show*, and the *Today Show*. They performed on the soundtrack and appeared in the MGM movie, *Overboard*, starring Goldie Hawn and Kurt Russell.

Current band members Tom and Tim Wright, John McDowell, and Greg Anderson are still very active in the music business.

THE WRIGHT BROTHERS
Left to right: Tom Wright, Ronnie Milsap, Karl Hinkle and Tim Wright

THE WRIGHT BROTHERS (1980)

Left to right: Tom Wright, Karl Hinkle and Tim Wright

Zerfas

ZERFAS (1973)
Left to right: Bryan Zerfas, Billy Rice, Mark Tribby, Dave Zerfas and Steve Newbold

Group members include:

Steve Newbold
Billy Rice
Mark Tribby
Bryan Zerfas
Dave Zerfas

Formed in 1973, this Indianapolis band began as the group Zerfas. They later became part of the group Jubal. A rare recording produced in 1973 (a small quantity was pressed) has become a popular collector's item. This album was recorded on the 700 West label. Other prerecorded 1970s recordings recently resurfaced included musicians Paul McBee and the Wright Brothers' vocalist Karl Hinkle. Collectors continue to search for them.

1970 Notables

Allison Turner

Calvin Turner

Charles Cotton

Harrison Turner

James Dixon

Melvin Turner

Michael Boards

Paul Turner

Rudy Ross

Ted Patterson

Toby Myers

The
Emphatic
Eighties

The Emphatic Eighties

Ronald Reagan's election as the 40th President of the United States over Jimmy Carter eased the country into the 1980s. George Bush was Vice President and former Nixon loyalist General Alexander Haig became Secretary of State when George Schultz resigned.

Relations between Israel and the U.S. were rocked when spy Jonathan Jay Pollard was exposed while passing secret security documents to America's ally. A Federal judge, unmoved by Pollard's passion to save Israel from doom, imposed a life sentence. Rallies were conducted across the country protesting Pollard's treatment.

President Reagan called the Soviet Union "The Evil Empire," and supported Central American rebels fighting for freedom. A scandal occurred when the president and other members of his administration were criticized for their part in what became known as "The Iran/Contra Affair." Regardless, Reagan trounced Walter Mondale to earn a second term in office in 1984.

A year later, terrorism reared its ugly head when the Italian oceanliner *The Achille Lauro* was seized. Four hundred and fifty passengers were held hostage, including an American who was executed.

In 1988, George Bush and Indiana-born Dan Quayle ascended to the White House by defeating Michael Dukakis and Lloyd Bentsen.

Cultural news was headlined when *Ordinary People* won the Academy Award for Best Picture in 1980. Robert De Niro won best actor for *Raging Bull*, and Sissy Spacek won best actress for her role in *Coal Miner's Daughter*. That film was based on the life story of country singer Loretta Lynn. Other films of note during the '80s included *An American Werewolf in London, An Officer and A Gentleman, Raiders of the Lost Ark, Amadeus,* and *Dirty Dancing. Hill Street Blues* became the number one television program.

Popular songs during the 1980s included, "Bettie Davis Eyes," "Abracadabra," "Jack & Diane," and "Flashdance." Indiana-born Michael Jackson contributed such hits as "Bad," "Thriller," and "Beat It."

In 1981, the music industry lost three icons when Bill Haley, Harry Chapin and Hoosier Hoagy Carmichael, composer of "Stardust," died. Celebrities such as John Belushi, Count Basie, and Muddy Waters also died during this decade.

During the 1980s, music flourished in Indiana. Michael Jackson's fame ignited interest in other Hoosier musicians. The styles varied, but famed groups such as Motley Crue and Guns N' Roses featured Indiana talent. Folk singer Carrie Newcomer gained attention, as did the three Mitchell sisters performing as The Starlettes. John Mellencamp continued to perform hit music, and Henry Lee Summer was popular, as were the jazz-rock group The Mathematicians, the Dancing Cigarettes, and Dow Jones and the Industrials.

Top nightspots in Indiana during the '80s included the Vogue, Bentley's, The Razz-Ma-Tazz, the Enterprise, the Sundance, and the Patio. These clubs provided the springboard for Indiana artists with an eye on the national spotlight. Those that performed during *The Emphatic Eighties* include:

Acid Green

ACID GREEN (1988)

Left to right: Gym Stoffer, Gregg Stewart, John Zeps, Sander Leech and Bob Cripe

Group members include:

Bob Cripe
Sander Leech
Gregg Stewart
Gym Stoffer
John Zeps

This heavy metal band was formed in Indianapolis in 1987 and continued to perform into the mid-1990s. They recorded one EP titled, *As The World Turns* (1991) on Rusty Low Records, and a CD *Nuciei* (1994) on Augmented Mammaet Records.

After 7

AFTER 7

Group members include:

Kevon Edmonds
Melvin Edmonds
Keith Mitchell

Formed in 1989 by Indiana University students, After 7 became one of Indiana's most successful R&B/Soul acts. They recorded their first album, self-titled *After 7* (1989), on the Virgin label. That recording produced four top 10 U.S. singles, and won a Grammy nomination for Best Soul Group. Their second recording, *Taking My Time* (1992), was also recorded on the Virgin label. Although not listed as one of the members, brother Kenny "Babyface" Edmonds contributed to the first recording. Edmonds returned in 1995 to write three songs, and sing "Honey, Oh How I Need You," for the group's third album, *Reflections*.

Big Twist And The Mellow Fellows

Group members include:

Big Twist (Larry Nolan)
Terry Ogolini
Pete Special

Born in Terre Haute in 1938, Larry Nolan performed under the name Big Twist. He was drummer and vocalist for the 1950s band Mellow Fellows. In the 1970s, this group performed behind artists such as James Brown and Big Joe Turner, and recorded on the Flying Fish Records and Alligator Records labels. In the 1980s, Nolan recorded several albums under the Big Twist name, including *Big Twist and The Mellow Yellows* and *Big Twist Playing For Keeps* (1993) on Alligator Records. *One Track Mind* on Red Lightnin,' and *Live from Chicago* (1987), returning to the Alligator label. Larry Nolan died of a heart attack March 14, 1990 in Broadview, Illinois.

Blue Print

Group members include:

Johnny Atkins
Mark Bullock
Mike Kopacek
Mark Steinhardt
Kenny Neal
Bobby Toon

Beki Brindle (Scala)

PHOTO CREDIT: LARRY GOSHEN

BEKI BRINDLE

Indiana native Beki Brindle grew up playing guitar with blues legend James "Yank" Rachell. She was guitarist for the Warner/Reprise band Grace Pool and toured with classic rocker Jerry Lee Lewis. While living in Ireland, she created and ran a blues workshop on Irish National television. Returning to the U.S., she made legendary recordings with "Yank" Rachell and several albums under her own name. Her recording of *All Kinds of Beki* was released in 2016 on Random Chance Records. As a New York Blues Hall of Fame inductee, Beki (Scala) Brindle continues to perform and live in New York City.

Cousins From Venus

Group members include:

Jennifer Ayers
Tim Ayers
Sarge Glanton
Mark Kennedy
Peabody

Other members include: Sreya Chambers, Czm and Johnny Vulcan.

The Dancing Cigarettes

Group members include:

Emily Bonus
Michael Gitlin
Timothy Noe
Jacklyn Oddi
John Terrill
G. Don Truboy

This Bloomington-based band was formed in 1980. They recorded one EP titled *Dancing Cigarettes* (1981) on the Gulcher label.

PHOTO CREDIT: JIMMY MACK

DELIVERANCE (1987)
Front row, left to right: Bill Ellis and Keith Phelps. Back row, left to right: James Fountain, Kevin Resnover, Kenny Phelps, Mark Plummer and Emmanuel Officer

Deliverance

Group members include:

Bill Ellis
James Fountain
Emmanuel Officer
Keith Phelps
Kenny Phelps
Mark Plummer
Kevin Resnover

Formed in 1987, this Indianapolis Gospel/Soul group recorded many gospel songs. Singer Emmanuel Officer later became a member of Kenny "Babyface" Edmonds' group, Manchild. Drummer Kenny Phelps and his brother Keith recorded backup for such groups as El Debarge.

Dow Jones And The Industrials

Group members include:

Dave Behnke

Chris Clark

Brad Garton

Greg Horn

Tim North

Jenny Sweany

This was a West Lafayette-based group that recorded one self-titled EP on the Gulcher label (1980).

THE LETTERMEN
Left to right: Donovan Scott Tea, Darren Dowler and Tony Butala

Darren Dowler

DARREN DOWLER

Indianapolis-born Darren Dowler grew up in a musical family. Darren's father, Danny Dollar (Dowler) began performing in the late 1950s. His mother Darlene, who also performed in the late 1950s, fronted her own band and entertained at some of the top nightspots in Florida. After moving to Daytona Beach, Darren started his musical career by singing at the age of fourteen. At the age of eighteen, he moved to Westport, Connecticut, where he formed his own group, the Darren Dowler Band.

Darren also entered the acting field and performed in the musical, *Grease*. He later landed small rolls in such television shows as *The Swamp Thing*, *The Adventures of Superboy* and *As The World Turns*. In the 1980s, Darren performed with his mother's band, Tyme, and in the 1990s joined the national singing group The Lettermen. Dowler later became a permanent member of Paul Revere's Raiders and continued to tour with the Oldies Concerts.

TYME
Left to right: Darlene (Dowler) Grigsby, Darren Dowler, Brian, Lea, Ken and Rob

An author of two novels, he continues his acting career by producing and staring in his own movies, already released, *Christmas In Hollywood* and *Rock and Roll the Movie*. As of this writing he will be displaying his acting skills portray the part of Billy Graham in a soon to be released movie, *Grace of The Father*.

The Equalizers

THE EQUALIZERS 91985)
Left to right: Glenn Cornick, Jinx Dawson and Michael Monarch

Group members include:

Glen Cornick
Jinx Dawson
Michael Monarch
Linda Nardini
Steve Ross

Indianapolis natives, and ex-Coven members Jinx Dawson and Steve Ross formed this Los Angeles band in the mid-1980s. The group also featured bass player Glen Cornick, a former member of Jethro Tull, and Michael Monarch, guitarist from the Steppenwolf band.

The First Impression

THE FIRST IMPRESSION (1986)
*Left to right: Jeff Reed, Wendy Auscherman, Kevin McDonald and
Steve Matthews*

Group members include:

Wendy Auscherman
Steve Matthews
Kevin McDonald
Jeff Reed

This band from the Indianapolis area was formed in 1985. They performed at local nightspots and special events. Their unique form of jazz and dance music earned them popularity. The band continued to perform, but not with the original members.

The Girls

Group members include:

Beau Brinkley
Julie Gerard
Bea Isaacs
Pam Lee
Kelly Oliver

The girls were originally formed in 1985 by bassist Bea Isaacs, guitarist Julie Gerard, and drummer Kelly Oliver. Pam Lee joined them in 1986 and Beau Brinkley became a member in 1987. The popular all-girl band toured the United States and Canada, and once a year, from 1987 through 1992, was booked into one of the top nightclubs in Las Vegas. In 1999, The Girls changed their name to Drama Queen, and recorded their first CD.

Group Theropy

Group members include:

Albert Bearman
John Dinwiddie
Mike Pipes
Jimmy Williams

Composing the original line-up of Group Theropy were Albert Bearman, Danny Daubkins, Mark Iverson, Kim Madget and Bruce Wiengart. The members in the photograph played together in 1988. This unit stayed together for two years, but Group Theropy, with different members, lasted into the 1990s. Starting out as an R&B Motown-style band, the group later worked into the top 40 rock 'n' roll market.

PHOTO CREDIT: JIMMY MACK

GROUP THEROPY
Left to right: Jimmy Williams, Albert Bearman, John Dinwiddie and Mike Pipes

Guns N' Roses

This heavy-metal band was formed in Los Angeles by two Indiana musicians, Axl Rose (William Bailey) and Issy Stradlin (Jeff Isbell). Both were born in Lafayette, Indiana. In 1986, Guns n' Roses recorded *Appetite For Destruction* on the Geffen label. It reached number one on the Billboard charts for five weeks and was a staple on the charts for nearly three years. The band continued to be popular in the 1980s and '90s, despite controversy between the performers and the media. The band's membership has changed many times since the early 1990s, with Rose and Reed as the only two constant members since 1990.

Barbara Higbie

Michigan-born Barbara Higbie was raised in Speedway, Indiana. After studying classical piano at the age of thirteen, she moved with her family to Ghana, West Africa. Barbara began her professional music career in the early 1980s in the San Francisco Bay area. She performed with artists such as Darol Anger, Mike Marshall, Todd Phillips, David Balakrishnan and Rob Wasserman.

In 1982, Barbara recorded *Tideline* on the Windham Hill label with violinist Darol Anger. She recorded an album with Teresa Trull titled *Unexpected* (1983). The *Boston Globe* named it as one of the ten best albums of the year. In 1985, Barbara recorded at the Montreux Jazz Festival in Switzerland with violinist Darol Anger. The recording on the Windham Hill label included Mike Marshall, Todd Phillips and Andy Narell. The group successfully recorded three albums under the Montreux name.

PHOTO CREDIT: IRENE YOUNG

BARBARA HIGBIE (1982)

Barbara earned a Grammy nomination for one of her own compositions. She has performed and recorded on over 40 albums, and in 1990 recorded a solo album on the Windham Hill label, *Signs Of Life*. It was named one of the ten best albums of the year by the *Washington Post*. Other recordings of note are *Barbara Higbie — I Surrender* (1996), and *Playtime* (1997) with Barbara Higbie and Teresa Trull, both on Slow Baby Records. Barbara Higbie lives in the San Francisco area and still tours nationally and internationally.

HOWARD & THE PERFECT ALIBI (1981)

Left to right: Doug Babb, Rick Taylor, Marci Parker, Howard Phillips, Suzi Love, Gary "Keith" Kincaid, Jeff Frazier. In Broad Ripple at the Patio Lounge with dancers.

Hugo Smooth Band

Group members include:

Ron Brinson
Joan E. Hall
Wayne Hall
Brian E. Paulson

This Indiana group from 1980 recorded one album, the self-titled *Hugo Smooth Band,* on the Big Time Records label.

Illicit Affair

PHOTO CREDIT: RICK CHILDRESS

ILLICIT AFFAIR (1983)

Front row, left to right: Ron Coffman and Dean Childress. Back row, left to right: Brad Estes, Jeff Holt and Jim Gardner

Group members include:

Dean Childress
Ron Coffman
Jay Davis
Brad Estes
Jim Gardner
Jeff Holt

This band from the Fowler, Indiana, area was formed in 1983. They recorded two 45s, "Girls In The USA"/"Leather Jacket On" (1984) and "History Is Made At Night"/"You Move Me" (1985).

Janet Jackson

Janet was born on May 16, 1966 in Gary. She began performing at the age of seven with her famous brothers, The Jackson 5. At age ten, Jackson played the television character Penny Gordon on the popular show *Good Times.*

In 1982, Janet recorded her first hit "Young Love" on the A&M label. Later in the 1980s and '90s, Janet was popular with her top R&B hit recordings *Control* (1986), *Rhythm Nation 1814* (1989) and *Janet* (1993). She also acted in the film, *Poetic Justice,* in 1983.

Janet continues to perform on tour, and in 2001, released the CD *All For You* on the Virgin label.

JANET JACKSON

La Toya Jackson

Born in Gary in 1956, La Toya Jackson was the fifth oldest child in the Jackson family. Her professional music career started around 1975 when she joined The Jacksons after they left Motown and regrouped. She recorded three albums in the 1980s, *La Toya Jackson, My Special Love* on Polydor Records, and *Heart Don't Lie* for the Private label. One of LaToya's original songs, "Reggae Night" was recorded by Jimmy Cliff and became a huge success in France. In 2018 at the age of 62, LaToya is still very active in the entertainment world.

LA TOYA JACKSON

Jubal Band

JUBAL BAND (1981)
*Left to right: Steve Newbold, Dave Zerfas, Howard Phillips,
Bryan Zerfas and John Dinwiddie*

Group members include:

John Dinwiddie
Steve Newbold
Howard Phillips
Bryan Zerfas
Dave Zerfas

This group is a later version of Jubal that was formed in 1981. This band had originated in the 1970s. In 2018, Singer Howard Phillips continued to perform with his own band, Howard and the Perfect Alibi.

Kilo

Group members include:

Charles
John Engelland
Georgia
Shawn Pelton
Dave Randle
Jeffrey Stuart
Crystal Taliefero

Formed in the mid-1980s, this funk-rock band was based in Bloomington. Some members were students at Indiana University and were involved in the Soul Review, a student jazz music organization. Member Crystal Taliefero recorded with Billy Joel and then toured with Bob Seger.

The Last Four (4) Digits

Group members include:

S.V. Gridgesby
J. Huffaker
J. Koss
Mr. Science
M. Sheets
R. Worth
XAX

This Indianapolis Punk Rock group was formed in 1981. They recorded one EP titled *Big Picture* on the Hardly Record label. In 2017, they reunited to perform and released an anthology of their past recordings titled *Don't Move* on Time Change Records.

Latex Novelties

Group members include:

Randy Creep
Otis Jayne Mansfield
Nox
Peter Pills
Andy Reyia

The repertoire of this 1985 avant-garde band from the Indianapolis area consisted of original material. Their odd fashion sense and strange song titles created a wide following.

LIGHT (1984)

Light

Group members include:

Jeff Hornbeck
Jeff Lance
John W. McDowell, III
Steve Walker

An Indianapolis band from the 1980s.

Malachi

MALACHI

Front row, left to right: John Dinwiddie, Kevin (Flash) Ferrell and Charley Grahn. Back row, left to right: Danny Williams, Robin Steele, Herald Gooch and Ricky Knox.

Group members include:

John Dinwiddie
Kevin "Flash" Ferrell
Herald Gooch
Charley Grahn
Ricky Knox
Robin Steele
Danny Williams

Indianapolis-based Malachi was originally formed in the early 1970s. The group in the photograph comprised the 1985 version. Malachi played the Indiana area, performing at proms, private functions and appearing occasionally at the popular Vogue nightclub.

Macumba Dentists

Group members include:

Kevin Kaiser
Bill Levin
Johnny Quest
Robin Reuter
Captain Steele

Mick Mars

(Bob Deal/Motley Crue)

Mick Mars, a/k/a Bob Deal, was born April 3, 1956 in Terre Haute. In the early 1980s, Mick placed a classified advertisement in the *Los Angeles Times* that read "Loud Rude Aggressive Guitarist Available." Band members contacted him and he began to play guitar and vocalize with the newly formed Motley Crue. The band included Tommy Lee (Bass) on drums. The heavy metal band climbed to the charts with *Shout at the Devil* (1983), *Theatre of Pain* (1985) and *Girl, Girls, Girls* (1987). Mick Mars continues to perform with Motley Crue. They released a reunion album, *Generation Swine* (1997), that climbed to the #5 position on the pop charts.

This Indianapolis-based band was formed in the 1980s.

MOTLEY CRUE
Third from left: Mick Mars (Bob Deal)

Mathematicians

Group members include:

Bob Fields
Eddy Humphrey
Kevin Kouts
Larry McCullough

This jazz-fusion rock group from the Indianapolis area was formed in 1989. Their recording of *Factor Of Four* (1996) included guest artists Cathy Morris on violin and Yun Hui on keyboards.

MATHEMATICIANS (1989)
Left to right: Kevin Kouts, Bob Fields, Larry McCullough and Eddy Humphrey

Carrie Newcomer

Carrie Newcomer was born in Elkhart, Indiana. She wrote her first song after graduating high school. During college, while studying visual arts, she paid her dues by performing in bars and bowling alleys. After college, she taught music during the day and spent her evenings doing what she loved best, performing.

In the mid-1980s, Carrie performed with the Lafayette band Stone Soup. She recorded two albums with that group before leaving in 1989 to pursue her own career.

CARRIE NEWCOMER

Carrie recorded her first solo album on the Windchime label in 1991 titled *Visions and Dreams.* She currently records for Rounder Records.

Carrie has opened nationally for artists such as Alison Krauss & Union Station, and has performed at Carnegie Hall and the London Royal Festival Theatre.

Carrie Newcomer is an extraordinary song writer who pens her songs from personal experience and the experiences of others.

John O'Banion

Kokomo native John O'Banion recorded two albums: a self-titled release in 1981 and *Danger* (1982), both on the Elektra label. His release of a single in 1981 titled "I Love You Like I Never Loved Before" climbed into the top 100 on the Billboard charts.

The Panics

Group members include:

Eric White

John Barge

Mike Ost

Johnny Carson

This Bloomington-based band recorded one EP, *The Panics* (1980) on the Gulcher (201) label.

The Passion

Group members include:

"Riley" Gary Anderson

Bruce Coombs

Mike Hall

Butch Sandlin

Joe Schreiner

Port Rasin Band

Group members include:

Jeff Martin

Jim Te Ronde

Brian Wooldridge

Scott Wooldridge

This band was formed in the early 1980s in Kokomo. Two members, Brian and Scott Wooldridge composed the soundtrack for the television series, *Party of Five*.

P.S. DUMP YOUR BOYFRIEND (1985)

P.S. Dump Your Boyfriend

Group members include:

Kevin Baxter
Dave Holcomb
Rick Long
Oliver Morris
Phil Pierle

Rastabilly Rebels

Group members include:

Randy Creep
Mark Cutsinger
Captain Steele
Bruce Stuckey
Thom Woodward

Recordio

Group members include:

Rick Clayton
Don Main
Mark Moran
Chris Pyle

Recordio was formed in Indianapolis around the mid-1980s. Formally called The Late Show, this group played original material, top 40, and classic R&B.

Red Beans & Rice

Group members include:

Tom Beckiehimer
Ed Jarman
Billy Young
Yun Hui

Red Beans & Rice was formed in 1989 in Indianapolis. Fronted by vocalist and keyboardist Yun Hui, the band played a progressive style of rhythm & blues. Yun Hui (pronounced Uni) is a native of South Korea and moved to the United States at the age of seven. After studying classical voice and piano at Indiana University, Yun Hui traveled around the United States for three years before returning to Indiana.

Red Bean & Rice recordings include *Staples* (1993), *Eat Big* (1996), *Yes We Can* (1999) and *Live Hot Beans* (2001). Red Beans & Rice disbanded in 2001, and Yun Hui relocated to Hollywood, California. Other members of this group were Robert Coleman, Jr., Darren Stroud and Jeff Triwedi.

RED BEANS & RICE (1989)
Front row, left to right: Billy Young and Ed Jarman. Back row, left to right: Tom Beckiehimer and Yun Hui.

Rods And Cones

Group members include:

P.K. Lavengood
Russ Levitt
Dave Post Merris

Originator P.K. Lavengood performed with several local bar bands in the early 1980s, including the band Safari. He later played with the Joe Ely Band, Storyville and John Mellencamp. Rods and Cones was formed in Bloomington in 1984. They opened for many big name artists, including Stevie Ray Vaughn. They recorded an EP in the 1980s, and produced a video titled *Boys Will Be Boys*. It received airplay on MTV.

John "BJ" Rogers

JOHN "BJ" ROGERS (1985)

Originally from Oregon, Rogers spent most of his later years in Indianapolis. A self-taught guitarist, Rogers was quite successful performing rock-a-billy and rock 'n' roll oldies. He traveled the country as a performing artist. In 1985, he appeared at the Buddy Holly Convention in Texas. His recording of "Buddy Holly Days"/"49 Lincoln" (1985) on Fraternity Records is rapidly becoming a collector's item. Other recordings include a CD, *Tech-No Colour* (1995), on Rivertown Records.

R.S.V.P.

R.S.V.P.
Left to right: Danny Brown, Kent Weineke, Scott Bailey and Brian Christopher

Group members include:

Scott Bailey
Danny Brown
Brian Christopher
Kent Weineke

This Indianapolis band performed on the local nightclub circuit in the 1980s. One of the members, Scott Bailey, is the son of Delbert Bailey, a popular singer from the 1960s and '70s.

Sally's Dream

Group members include:

Jenny Davis
Chris Dickinson
Cyn Hammond
Emily Jackson

In 1985, this Bloomington-based rock band received rave reviews while performing on the local nightclub scene. Opening for national acts, they worked in such clubs as the Second Story and Jake's.

The Starlettes (The Fabulous Starlettes)

Group members include:

Julie Mitchell
Mary Mitchell
Zanna Mitchell

This popular 1980s sister trio was in great demand around the Indianapolis area. Their showmanship and zeal for singing made the Starlettes stand out as performers. Zanna later became a member of the popular Alligator Brothers band, Zanna Doo. Recently (2018) she has been performing with singer Henry Lee Summer.

THE STARLETTES (1985)
Left to right: Julie Mitchell, Mary Mitchell, Zanna Mitchell

Carl Storie

Left to right: Mark Cawley, John Cascella, Bill Brunt and Carl Storie

Carl Storie was born in Muncie and attended Ball State University. In the mid-1960s, while attending high school, Carl watched The Beatles at the Indianapolis Coliseum. Inspired by the performance, Carl and his friends sold their prized possessions to purchase musical instruments. He then formed the group Chosen Few. After recording a few singles on the Denim and Talum labels, the group was signed by RCA. Carl performed with such groups as Limousine, The Faith Band and the Alligator Brothers, and in 1999 released his own CD. In 2018, he continues to entertain in the Indianapolis area with The Naptown Royals.

HENRY LEE SUMMER

Henry Lee Summer

Popular singer and musician Henry Lee Summer was born on July 5, 1955 in Brazil, Indiana. A self-taught musician on the drums, piano and guitar, he became a top entertainer. Summer performed in many of the top nightclubs throughout the Midwest. In 1982 he released his first single "Sweet Love." In 1984, he recorded his first LP, *Stay With Me*, and in 1985 released *Time For Big Fun*. In 1988, Henry signed for CBS Associated Records and released the self-titled album *Henry Lee Summer*. That same year he appeared on MTV in his own music video. Other albums released by Summer were *I've Got Everything* (1989), *Way Past Midnight* (1991), *Slam Dunk* (1993), *Smoke And Mirrors* (1999), *Live* (2000) and *Big Drum* (2001). Some of the musicians who performed in the Henry Lee Summer band were Rick Bennick, John Cascella, John Gunnell, Debbie Lisotto, singer Mimi Mapes, Michael Organ and Michael Reed.

CARL STORIE

Sweetwater

SWEETWATER (1985)
Left to right: Mike Berry, Rocky Givans, Larry Goshen, Ray Choate and Perry Choate

Group members include:

Mike Berry
Perry Choate
Ray Choate
Rocky Givans
Larry Goshen

Not to be confused with the national group Sweetwater, this band was formed in 1980 in Indianapolis and played the local nightclub scene. Sweetwater played a mixture of music that borders on country and top 40 rock & roll. In the 1990s, singer Mike Berry recorded one CD single which included Sweetwater's musicians Perry Choate, Larry Goshen and guest violinist Cathy Morris. The band performed at Bob's Midway in Greenwood for many years. Other members of the group included Marden Baker, Gary Coan, Paul Hutchinson, Gary Jacobsen and John Shaver. Today the Sweetwater band has been revised by dummer T Tommy Smith and includes two original members, Mike Berry and Gary Jacobsen.

Crystal Taliefero

Crystal Taliefero was born in Bourne, Massachusetts, and raised in Hammond, Indiana. She first started performing at the age of eleven. While in her early teens, she performed with her brother in the group Magic Mist. This group opened for such acts as The Staple Singers, Deniece Williams and Gladys Knight and the Pips. While attending Indiana University, she joined the band Kilo, and then was recruited by John Mellencamp for the national *Scarecrow* tour.

While touring in Los Angeles, she was spotted by singer Bob Seger. After the Mellencamp tour was completed, she joined Seger to play saxophone and percussion, and contribute to background vocals. Crystal later returned to Bloomington in 1987 to perform on John Mellencamp's album *The Lonesome Jubilee*. She has recorded with Billy Joel and toured with such artists as The Bee Gees and Bruce Springsteen.

Thrust

Group members include:

Tim Berry
Steve Delong
Mark Galster
Curt Robinette
Mike Sullivan

This top 40 band was formed in the mid-1980s. They performed original material earning them popularity on the nightclub circuit. They entertained at the Vogue in Indianapolis and toured throughout the Midwest.

Toxic Reason

Group members include:

Terry Howe
Rob Lucjak
J.J. Pearson
Ed Pittman
Greg Stort
Bruce Stuckey

Voices

Group members include:

Dave Derrikson
Bryan Disbro
Elliott Jackson
Billy Mercury
Wanda Micheli
Dallas Miller
Rusty Sapp

Formed in 1983, this Indianapolis band worked the nightclub circuit and performed top 40 and original material. Other members of this group were Rick Alexander and Joe Bishop.

WHY ON EARTH

Why On Earth

Group members include:

Mark Cutsinger
Dwayne Kendall
Mickey Mace
Jason Stonewall
Joe Joe Weekend

This Indiana group was formed in the mid-1980s. They recorded one self-titled LP, *Why On Earth* (1985).

Wildfire

PHOTO CREDIT: LARRY GOSHEN

WILDFIRE (1985)
*Left to right: John Scott, Paul Hutchinson, Dave Elmore,
Gary Jacobsen, Dave Martin and Jackie Jacobsen.
(Not pictured: Bill Kirkpatrick and Mike Berry.)*

Group members include:

Mike Berry
Dave Elmore
Paul Hutchinson
Gary Jacobsen
Jackie Jacobsen
Bill Kirkpatrick
Dave Martin
John Scott

This short-lived band was formed in 1985. They were finalists in the Marlboro Country Music Contest of the same year.

The Naughty Nineties

The Naughty Nineties

The Bill Clinton era pervaded the persona of the 1990s. The unlikely successor to George Bush became a controversial president whose regime would be rocked with personal scandal. Regardless, he became the only sitting president to play the saxophone!

Prior to Clinton's residence in the White House, George Bush dueled with Iraqi madman Saddam Hussein. After Saddam decided Kuwait was to his liking and invaded the country, Bush countered with American might in the Gulf War. Superior firepower permitted Bush to win, but he never snuffed out Saddam, who would continue to be a thorn in the side of the United States for the remainder of the decade and beyond.

America's previous archenemy, the Soviet Union, became embattled in economic strife and relations thawed as new countries in that region were established. In the United States, the economy flourished and millions became wealthy through investment in the Internet. The term, "Dot-Comers" was added to the vocabulary to indicate those who believed that cyberspace was the space of the future.

Films that were popular as the '90s began included *Dick Tracy, Teenage Mutant Ninja Turtles,* and *Good Fellas. Married With Children* became a wacky way for television viewers to view the modern family.

On the music scene, rap music was the rage and new groups like Boyz II Men and Spice Girls became popular. Madonna's recordings topped the charts and Michael Jackson and John Mellencamp continued to be headliners. The jazz world lost icons such as Miles Davis, Art Blakey, Gerry Mulligan, and Stan Getz.

The rock 'n' roll world mourned the passing of the gravelly voice disc jockey, Wolfman Jack. Stephen King novels such as *Misery* scared the bejesus out of readers. John Grisham books sold millions, and golfer Tiger Woods became a phenomenon.

Popular songs in the '90s included Whitney Houston's, "I Will Always Love You," MC Hammer's, "You Can't Touch This," "Ice Baby Ice," "Man In The Box," by Alice in Chains, "November Rain" by Guns N' Roses, and "Black or White" by Michael Jackson.

Since the 1990s produced so many different forms of music, Indiana musicians that recorded then vary as much as the type of clothes and hairstyles that filtered through the decade. One Indiana born and bred musician who made his mark was Kenneth "Babyface" Edmonds. His creative talent as a songwriter and producer boosted the careers of many artists. Others who contributed to the music scene included Cathy Morris, the popular jazz violinist who played fusion jazz/rock as well as Latin and classical.

Nightspots that heralded Indiana performers included The Patio and the Vogue as well as the Cozy, C.T. Peppers, and the Rathskeller. Jazz clubs such as the Chatterbox and the Jazz Kitchen were also quite popular. Outdoor venues such as Deer Creek, Circle Fest, Mid-Summer Fest, and Indiana's first national festival, the Indy Jazz Fest, flourished.

The 1990s was a "musical fest" famous for variety and new voices. Indiana musicians continued to play their part on the national and international scene. Included among those who performed during *The Naughty Nineties* were:

Babyface (Kenneth Edmonds)

Kenneth Edmonds was born in Indianapolis, Indiana on April 10, 1959. He began his music career in the 1970s with the Indiana group Manchild. He later joined his two brothers, Kevon and Melvin, in their R&B band After 7, and the Cincinnati group Steele with producing partner, Antonio "L.A." Reid.

Although most of his solo recording work is excellent, Babyface is most recognized for his achievements as a producer. By 1997, he had earned 116 top 10 R&B and pop hits, with 46 of them topping the R&B charts. One of Edmonds's productions, "End of the Road" by Boyz II Men, stayed at number one on the Billboard charts for 13 weeks.

With partner Reid, he produced hits for such artists as Toni Braxton, Bobby Brown, Whitney Houston, Boyz II Men, Eric Clapton, Brandy, Madonna and many others. To honor Edmonds, a stretch of I-65 southeast of Indianapolis is named for him.

The Beautiful Authentic Zoo Gods

Group members include:

Anthony Cooper
Scott David
Eric Grimmet
Lewis S. Jones
Jeff Ketron

This Indianapolis-based band recorded a CD titled *Birth* (1993) on the Los Angeles record label, Cleopatra.

Mike Berry

Indianapolis singer/guitarist Mike Berry performed with the Sweetwater band in the mid-1980s. After twelve years with Sweetwater, Berry recorded a CD featuring violinist Cathy Morris, titled *If We Were Gypsy's*. This 2-song CD was recorded on Reneé Records. The title track was written and produced by drummer Larry Goshen. The second song "Don't Ever Love Me Like That" was penned by Mike Berry. In 2018, he continued to perform in the Indianapolis area with a revised version of the Sweetwater band.

PHOTO CREDIT: LARRY GOSHEN

CATHY MORRIS & MIKE BERRY

Birdmen of Alcatraz

Group members include:

Dino Codalata "Googooma"
Russ Johnson "Choc"
Matthew Van Kersen "Skyskrapa"
Steve Wolf "Pappaw"

This Indianapolis rock band was formed in the 1990s. They recorded a song on the surf record label called Focus (1996).

Blaq Lily

Blaq Lily was formed in 1999 by the husband and wife team of Arminta and Raven. Arminta is a native of Lafayette, and Raven was born in Laurel, Indiana. Blaq Lily derived from the folk group Special Forces, and the gothic project titled LivingDead. This neo-celtic acoustic duo performs in Indianapolis and the surrounding area. They recorded their first CD in 1999 titled *Blaq Lily,* and thereafter released two more recordings.

BLAQ LILY

Phil T. Blues

From Kokomo, Phil Thompson recorded one CD, *The Original Kokomo Bluesman,* in 1996. He performed on the nightclub circuit in Kokomo, as well as at the popular Slippery Noodle in Indianapolis. Phil began his music career by performing with the group Heavy in the mid-1960s.

PHIL T. BLUES

Blind Otis & The Lost Highway

Group members include:

Jeff Downey
Dave Hooper
Nick "Sweet River" Jones
Blind Otis

This Indiana R&B blues band recorded one CD, *Fools Parade* (1996) on Freedom Machine Records.

Tim Brickley

Indianapolis-based Tim Brickley moved from San Francisco to Indiana in the mid-1970s. A graduate of North Central High School and Indiana University, Brickley became highly successful as a composer, performer and producer. He performed in the mid-1980s with Today's Icons and opened for such acts as Culture Club.

With his New York composing partner, David Rheins, he produced the CD, *Be Apart,* (1995). This recording featured Brickley with the Bleeding Hearts, a rock band formed in Indianapolis. In 1998, Brickley won an Emmy Award for Outstanding Achievement in Musical Composition for his score of the documentary *Hoosier Hoops: The Golden Era.* His song "Tangled and Tempted" was featured in the 1998 film release of *Going All The Way.*

TIM BRICKLEY

Brickley is well known for his jazz vocalizing with the Tim Brickley Quintet. He now operates his own recording studio and continues to perform at music venues in the Indiana area. Members of the Bleeding Hearts include Kevin Anker, Tad Armstrong, John Byrne and Steve Prince.

Buzzy Jones

BUZZY JONES

Group members include:

Steve Butcher
Greg Hedges
Richard Owens

This Indianapolis-based band recorded several CDs, including *Buzzy Jones* (1993) on Hipswervy Records, *Female Delight* (1995) and *To Helmsburg And Back* (1996) on Billy Boy Records.

Larry Calland (Conga Jazz)

LARRY CALLAND

Percussionist Larry Calland was originally from Toledo, Ohio, but has called Indianapolis his home since the mid-1990s. He performed briefly with the groups Beeble Brox and The Drums of West Africa. In the mid-1990s, Calland formed the group Conga Jazz. That group performed local concerts, and appeared at popular nightclubs such as the Chatterbox and Jazz Kitchen. In 1999, he recorded the CD *Spirit*.

Conga Jazz included musicians Robert Coleman, Dr. Virginia Jefferson, Bill Myers and saxophonist Kenny Kipp.

Larry Calland died on April 25, 2015.

Jan Aldridge Clark

Jan Aldridge Clark was born and raised in Detroit, Michigan, but resided in Indianapolis. The variety of Clark's musical ability as a harpist, including the ability to play jazz, separates her from others. She performed with her jazz trio at the popular Chatterbox. She can be heard on Keni Washington's recording of *Erosonata,* and her own recording in 2004 *Anything but Ordinary.* She continues to perform in the Indianapolis area.

PHOTO CREDIT: LARRY GOSHEN

JAN ALDRIDGE CLARK

Governor Davis & The Blues Ambassadors

Group members include:

Ron "R.C." Coffman
Governor Davis
Jose C. Joven
Steve Robbins

Originally from Chicago, Governor Davis calls Indianapolis his home. His first musical influences came from his father. He performed in Chicago's north-side nightclubs. Davis studied keyboards and received gospel influence from his Aunt Ollie, a church organist. The Blues Ambassadors performed a mixture of soul and R&B. In 1997, they recorded a CD titled *I Am The Governor.*

GOVERNOR DAVIS

KARA DAY

Kara Day

Indiana native Kara Day has been playing the violin since she was four years old. She has performed locally and nationally with such groups as the Indianapolis Symphony Orchestra, the Philharmonic of Fort Wayne and New Jersey, the Long Island Philharmonic, the New York Pops and the American Jazz Philharmonic. Kara has backed up such national acts as Elton John, James Taylor, Natalie Cole, Led Zeppelin and Sting, and has recorded with such local artists as Cathy Morris, Frank Glover and Cynthia Layne & Leta Essig. Kara Day is not only an accomplished violinist, but also a singer and writer who has performed and fronted her own rock band.

GENE DEER

Gene Deer

Blues singer Gene Deer was born and raised in Indianapolis. Deer began playing guitar at age twelve. By the age of fourteen, he was performing for friends in his neighborhood. He launched his professional career at age sixteen. In the mid-1980s, Deer performed with the rock band Coda, and in 1989 The Generators. In 1993, Deer won fourth place in the B.B. King National Blues Competition, and in 1995 recorded his first CD, *Soul Tender*. His recording, *Livin' With The Blues* (1998) was released on the Slippery Noodle label.

Jennie DeVoe

Muncie, Indiana native Jennie DeVoe was raised in a musical family. While being nurtured by that environment, she entered the world of entertainment. After working with the Larry Crane band (John Mellencamp's guitarist), and the No Regrets blues group, Jennie recorded voice-overs for radio commercials. In 1998, her original song "Red Hot Sun" won Honorable Mention in the John Lennon Songwriting Contest. In 1999, she made a personal appearance with Dick Clark, and was inducted into the American Bandstand Hall of Fame. Jennie has recorded several CDs under her own name, *Does She Walk On Water* (1998), *Ta Da* (2000), *Thank You Goodnight* (2002), *Firewerks & Kurate Supplies* (2004), and *Strange Sunshine* (2009) all on the Rubin The Cat label. As of 2018, Jennie DeVoe continues to perform in the Indiana area.

PHOTO CREDIT: LARRY GOSHEN

JENNIE DeVOE

Dog Talk

Group members include:

Michael Beck
Cliff Fortney
Bill Lancton
Jim Litchfield
Cliff White

Indianapolis group Dog Talk performed a unique blend of World Music — calypso, pop, reggae, rock, Latin and zydeco. They have performed in clubs around the Midwest. Dog Talk has opened for such acts as Bonnie Raitt, Bruce Hornsby, Phish, and Buckwheat Zydeco. Their debut CD titled, *It Happens Every Day* (1995), was recorded live at the popular Indianapolis club, the Jazz Kitchen.

DOG TALK

Steve Dokken

Steve Dokken is well known in the Midwest as one of the finest bass musicians. Raised in Minneapolis, Dokken moved to Indianapolis in the late 1970s. He performed with Henry Mancini from 1979 until Mancini's death in 1994. Dokken has performed with Rod Stewart, Moody Blues, Natalie Cole, Johnny Mathis and many others.

Through the latter part of the 1990s and early 2000s, Steve Dokken recorded and performed with popular jazz violinist Cathy Morris. Dokken continues to be active in perfoming concerts and recording work.

PHOTO CREDIT: LARRY GOSHEN

STEVE DOKKEN

Steve Dokken   Jack Gilfoy   Cecil Welch   Royce Campbell   Henry Mancini   Al Cobine

Drama Queen

Group members include:

Beau Brinkley
Julie Gerard
Bea Isaacs
Pam Lee
Kelly Oliver

This all-girl group performed in the 1980s under the name The Girls. In 1999, after re-forming (with all original members), they have become one of Indiana's most popular all-female bands. Their recording, the self-titled *Drama Queen*, received much airplay in the Hoosier State.

DRAMA QUEEN

Leta Essig (Gentry)

Indianapolis-born singer Leta Essig has performed in many theatre stage productions, including the popular Footlight Musicals. She recorded backup vocals for many artists, including the final release of the late Bobby Helms. Leta performed a long stint with the popular group Trina & The Gypsies.

In 1999, she teamed up with singer Cynthia Layne for the showcase album, *Just For A Thrill*. She performed with the band Sequel, and as of 2018 provides vocals for the rock-pop, R&B/disco group Tastes Like Chicken.

PHOTO CREDIT: LARRY GOSHEN

LETA ESSIG

Ronnie Haig Band & The Pletchers

Group members include:

Gilbert Gordon
Larry Goshen
Ronnie Haig
Paul Hutchinson

The Pletchers group members include:

Carla Sue Pletcher
Roxie Pletcher

This showcase group became the first house band and opening act at the Fountain Room, located in the historic Fountain Square Theatre building in Indianapolis. The Fountain Room opened in 1994. It showcased the sounds of the 1950s and '60s.

This band featured recording artist Ronnie Haig and back up singers, sisters Roxie and Susie Pletcher. Roxie is an accomplished songwriter. Keyboardist and singer Carla Sue (Susie) is married to Haig and is an assistant in his home recording studio.

The band previously featured keyboardist Gilbert Gordon, who released his own CD, *Double or Nothin'*, in 1997, and saxophonist Paul Hutchinson, whose recording of *Saxy Moods* was released in 1998.

(Information on Ronnie Haig can be found in the 1950s section)

RONNIE HAIG BAND (1994)
*Left to right (top): Ronnie Haig, Gilbert Gordon and Paul Hutchinson,
with Larry Goshen in front.*

PHOTO CREDIT: LARRY GOSHEN

Left to right – Roxie Pletcher, Carla Sue Pletcher and Ronnie Haig

Monika Herzig & Peter Kienle

(Beeble Brox)

Monika and Peter were born and raised in Germany and moved to the United States around 1988. They have been permanent residents of Bloomington since 1991. Monika holds a Masters Degree in Music Education from the University of Alabama and a Doctorate in Music Education and Jazz Studies from Indiana University. Peter composes and arranges music and the two, in the 1990s, led the popular Bloomington jazz-fusion group, Beeble Brox. They have released several recordings including *Entropy* (1990), *The Thing* (1991), *Raw Material* (1994), *Quantumn Tweezers* (1995), *Indianapolis Intergalactic Spaceport* (1997) and *Dominanc Domain* (1998).

Peter also performed guitar on the Acme release, *3rd Man* (1998), with musicians Jack Helsley and Pete Wilhoit. In 2018, he was busy performing and recording with The Time Flies band that includes Quinn Sternberg, Josh Roberts and Monika Herzig.

Monika released a CD in 2000 titled *Monika Herzig Acoustic Project, Melody Without Words,* and then *Melody with Harmony* in 2003. Other recordings by Monika Herzig are *Jammin' At the Kitchen* (2001), *In Your Own Sweet Voice* (2004), *What Have You Gone and Done?* (2006), *Peace on Earth* (2008), *Come with Me* (2011), and in 2018, with her all-female group, *Sheroes.* She has two published books under her name *David Baker A Legacy in Music* and *Experiencing Chick Corea.*

PHOTO CREDIT: LARRY GOSHEN

MONIKA HERZIG

PHOTO CREDIT: LARRY GOSHEN

PETER KIENLE

SHANNON HOON (CENTER) WITH BLIND MELLON

Shannon Hoon

(Blind Mellon)

Born in Lafayette, Indiana, Shannon Hoon was the lead singer for the neo-pyschedelic/alternative rock group Blind Mellon. Formed in Los Angeles, California, they are best known for their 1993 single "No Rain." They toured with such groups as Neil Young and the Rolling Stones and performed at the 1994 edition of Woodstock. Shannon Hoon's stardom was cut short when he died on October 21, 1995 of an accidental drug overdose.

PHOTO CREDIT: LARRY GOSHEN

KEVIN JOHNSON

Kevin Johnson

Drummer Kevin Johnson was born in Brooklyn on April 22, 1951. Kevin's father is J.J. Johnson, one of the world's greatest jazz trombonists. Growing up in a musical family, Kevin began playing drums when he was six years old. He later performed for five years with Les McCann and made several recordings. Kevin toured with his father's band, and in the mid-1980s moved to Indianapolis. He performs regularly with his own band and fills in on drums with groups led by Oliver Nelson, Jr., Michael Brown and many others.

Cynthia Layne

Cynthia Layne was born in Dayton, Ohio, but had been a resident of Indianapolis for many years. A singer of jazz, soul, pop and R&B, Cynthia has appeared at some of Indy's top nightclubs, including the Jazz Kitchen and the Chatterbox, as well as many well-known clubs in Chicago and Cincinnati.

In 1999, Layne recorded a showcase CD with singer Leta Essig titled *Just For A Thrill* on Face The Music Records. In 2001, Cynthia released a CD titled *In Due Time,* in 2004 the recording *Reality* and 2007 *Beautiful Soul* on the Owl Records.

Cynthia passed away on January 18, 2015 at the age of 51 due to complacations of breast cancer.

PHOTO CREDIT: LARRY GOSHEN

CYNTHIA LAYNE

Ma Kelley

Group members include:

Cozy Johnson
Dan Metro
Terry Potts
Troy Seele
Bo Wallace

This Indianapolis band recorded five albums in the 1990s on the Surf Record label. Some were released on vinyl. Later recordings were pressed on CD. The recordings included the self-titled *Ma Kelley, Some Live, Some Not, Banned In America, Change In The Weather* and *Human Dance.*

Ann McWilliams

PHOTO CREDIT: LARRY GOSHEN

ANN McWILLIAMS

Singer-songwriter Ann McWilliams was born in Indianapolis and graduated from Lawrence Central High School. She appeared on the nationally televised *Jenny Jones Show,* and hosted her own radio program, *The City of Music Radio Hour.* She recorded and performed in the mid-1980s with Plaid Descent, and later released three CDs under her own name *Ann McWilliams* (1999), *Sister Luna & The Diamond Stars* (2001) and *Wrapped Around It* in 2003.

Mike Milligan & Steam Shovel

Group members include:
   Bob Brietung
   Brett Donovan
   Barry Kem
   Mike Milligan

Earlier members were:
   Eric Brown
   Patrick Glass

This Kokomo-based band was originally formed at Ball State University around 1993. Leader Mike Milligan was born and raised in Kokomo, and began playing guitar at the age of six. His father, Big Mike Milligan, was also a musician. He performed with the band Ramm, who opened for such national groups as the Drifters. Mike Milligan recorded one CD in 1998 titled *All My Life* on the Milligan Music label.

David Morgan

Born in Indianapolis, David Morgan has been involved in music since the early 1960s. During his time as a music instructor for IUPUI, he performed regularly at the popular blues club, the Slippery Noodle. Morgan's recordings include *I Never Knew She Was Married* (1993), *Pig Trader Blues* (1995), recorded with Yank Rachell, and *How Long Must I Wait For You* (1997).

Cathy Morris

Columbus, Indiana native Cathy Morris is one of the top jazz violinists in the country. After earning a degree from Indiana University in violin, she became successful as a performer and bandleader. Cathy and her band have opened for Al Jareau, Burt Bacharach, George Benson, Chuck Mangione, just to name a few. She has performed with such artists as David Baker, David Darling, Darol Anger and many others.

Performing with her own band she has toured Japan, played for President Bill Clinton, and recorded five CDs under her own name. Cathy's recordings include *Cathy Morris* (1993), *On The Run* (1994), *It's About Time* (1997), *A Cathy Morris Christmas* (1998), *Welcome To My World* (2001) and *Latin Jazz* (2005). She can be heard on *Myths For A New Millennium* (1999), Winton Reynolds CD, *Circles In Time* (2000), and Cynthia Layne and Leta Essig's recording of *Just For A Thrill* (1999).

PHOTO CREDIT: LARRY GOSHEN

CATHY MORRIS

Cathy Morris is a composer/arranger, and as a producer is credited for creating Arts With A Purpose, a non-profit organization connecting communities to artists to create positive individual and social change.

The Mysteries of Life

Group members include:

Tina Barbieri

Geraldine Haas

Freda Love

Jake Smith

A Bloomington-based band that recorded one CD, *Keep A Secret* (1996), for the RCA record label.

No Regrets

Group members include:

Wes Beam
Steve Brown
Jerome Mills
Kim Schilling

This Indianapolis-based band was very popular in the 1990s. At one time, they featured singer and recording artist, Jennie DeVoe.

Olive Lucy

Group members include:

Aaron Distler
Andrew Fish
Brandon Gibson
John Gibson
Leo Kempf
Mat Cartin
Amy Penrod
Robert Renock

Evansville, Indiana-based Olive Lucy recorded one CD, sthe elf-titled *Olive Lucy* (1998), on High Step Records.

Plaid Descent

PLAID DESCENT

Group members include:

Mark Bertram
Diane Ferguson
Ann McWilliams
Dave Pleiss

Plaid Descent was formed in 1993 in Indianapolis. This group featured two female singers/guitarists, Diane Ferguson and Ann McWilliams. Recordings include two CDs, *The Loud Quiet Ones* (1993) and *Plaid Descent* (1995).

Push Down & Turn

Group members include:

Jason Barth
Tay Bourquein
Jason Brown
Matt Devore
Sam King

In the early 1990s, this band was formed in Greencastle at DePauw University. Push Down & Turn has performed more than 1,600 performances, including the H.O.R.D.E. tour. They appeared on the main stage of X-Fest at Verizon Wireless Music Center in Noblesville. These performing close friends were togeter for ten years and recorded four popular albums in the '90s.

Jes Richmond

Group members include:

Phil Jacoby
Joey Means
Jes Richmond
Vicky Richmond
John Smotherman

This Shelbyville, Indiana band featured Shelbyville native Jes Richmond, and Vicky Richmond, originally from the St. Louis area. Jes performed nationally in Los Angeles and Denver, opening for such

JES RICHMOND

acts as Willie Nelson, Emmylou Harris, Jann Browne and the Desert Rose Band.

Vicky has appeared in several movies, and performed roles in television's *Dinah, General Hospital,* and *Moonlighting.*

The group's CD, *Full Circle,* was released in 1996. It received national airplay.

They continue to live and perform in the Florida area.

Roadhouse

ROADHOUSE

Group members include:

Craig Blattner
Eric Blattner
Jeff Gill
Kurtis Higgins
Doug McCoy
Michael McFarland
Bill Ritter
Paul Schafer
Ezra Todd Shelton

Drummer Kurtis Higgins formed Roadhouse in 1990. They performed cover tunes and original material at such clubs as the Slippery Noodle, and the Cozy in Indianapolis. In 2000, Roadhouse recorded a live CD titled *No Guarantees*. It was recorded live at Mickey's Irish Pub in Carmel.

Rozen Bombs

ROZEN BOMBS

Group members include:

Tom Beven
Jetta Cruse
Lisa Reimer

This band featured three talented musicians, Evansville's guitarist Tom Beven, who performed with groups C.O.D. and Quixotic Swordfish; Paducah, Kentucky's Jetta Cruse, a keyboardist, vocalist and bassist who got her start from her family's group, The Singing Cruses; and Ludington, Michigan native Lisa Reimer, who performed on drums and vocals and cites her influences as Buddy Rich and Neil Peart. They recorded one CD, *Like A Vaudeville Torpedo* (1997).

Sindacato

Group members include:

Frank Dean

Carl LoSasso

Jon Martin

Gary Wasson

The Indianapolis-based group Sindacato is best known as a "hillbilly soul band." That accounts for the airplay of their recordings on country and blues stations across the Midwest. The band was commended for their 1995 release of *Appalachian Pipeline*. It featured fiddle and mandolin player Jason Roller and musicians Frank Dean, Rory Harper, Allen Stratyner and Mark Kurkowski. Other known members of this group were Jim Crismore, Ralph Jeffers and Charlie Overton. Sindacato has opened for such acts as Emmylou Harris, George Jones, Todd Rundgren, Lynyrd Skynyrd and The Mavericks. They have performed for capacity audiences at Deer Creek and the Vogue in Indianapolis. In 1998, the group released their second CD, the self-titled *Sindacato,* on Union Records. Guitarist Frank Dean continues to perform with Sindacato and fronts the group Frank Dean & The Peterbuilts. This band features LuAnn Lietz, Kim Gradolf, Michael Wilson and Gene Trueblood.

Small Talk

Group members include:

Jim Albrecht

Jozell Carter

Clifford Ratliff

Gary Walters

David Young

This popular Indianapolis trio/quartet was formed from the 1980s jazz group Speakeasy. In 1995, Small Talk headlined local concerts, and performed in some of Indiana's top jazz clubs. Their CD, *In Spite Of It All* (1995) was recorded on the Forum Records label. This recording featured original compositions by saxophonist David Young and keyboardist Gary Walters.

SMALL TALK

Left to right, Jim Albrecht, Jozell Carter and Gary Walters

Charlie Smith

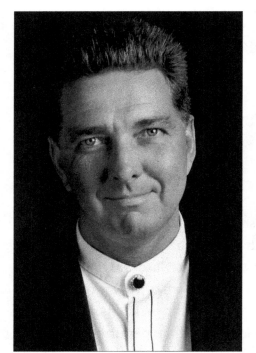

Guitarist/composer Charlie Smith was born in Anderson. He studied guitar at age sixteen. In the early 1970s, he formed the band Sojourn. In the '70s, he became a member of the group Jubal. Smith performed with Carl Storie & The Tornadoes in the 1980s. In the mid-1990s, he was a member of the jazz-fusion group, Timeout. Smith has performed with the Bob & Tom Band. In 1997, he appeared at the Montreux Jazz Festival with pianist Steve Allee. In 1999, he released the CD, *Absolutely.* It was named Best Smooth Jazz CD by *Nuvo Magazine.* Charlie Smith passed away in February of 2008.

CHARLIE SMITH

Frank Steans

Guitarist/singer Frank Steans was born in Chicago, Illinois, and raised in Anderson, Indiana. A long-time resident of Indianapolis, Frank entertained for more than thirty years, touring the country and performing for such artists as Marvin Gaye, The Staple Singers, The Dramatics and Milly Jackson. He performed regularly with the Clifford Ratliff jazz band at such clubs as the Jazz Kitchen.

PHOTO CREDIT: LARRY GOSHEN

FRANK STEANS

Rodney Stepp

Rodney Stepp was born in Indianapolis and graduated from Crispus Attucks High School. He first studied piano at age thirteen. At fifteen, he was performing for the Spinners. Rodney opened for many major acts and performed at the famous Cotton Club in Chicago, Illinois. He has been musician and conductor for Atlantic recording artists, The Spinners, Sister Sledge and Ronnie Dyson. Rodney's achievements include film soundtracks, commercials, recording productions and many awards. In 1997, he released the CD *Rodney Stepp & BSB, Steppin' Out,* on the Brooks Street Music label. He continues to perform as a member of the rock band Flying Toasters and with his own funk/jazz group The Steppin' Out Band.

RODNEY STEPP

Darren Stroud

Accomplished guitarist Darren Stroud was born in Orleans, Indiana. Stroud performed with musicians Yun Hui, Red Beans & Rice and his own band, The Darren Stroud Excursion. With the Excursion, Stroud opened for artists Ted Nugent, Bad Company and REO Speedwagon. Darren Stroud's guitar work can be heard on the Red Beans & Rice recordings, and on *Guitarboy Plays the Blues* (1999) and *Guitar Absolute* (2000) for the Yuni Vision label. Before moving to California in 2001, Stroud performed and recorded with Yun Hui in the techno rock group Meme.

PHOTO CREDIT: LARRY GOSHEN

DARREN STROUD EXCURSION
Left to right: Glen Hopkins, Tim Hunt and Darren Stroud

Timeout

Group members include:

Kevin Kaiser

Barry Kettery

Chris Pyle

Charlie Smith

Michael Stricklin

Gary Walters

This short-lived jazz/fusion group was one of the best in the Indianapolis area in the 1990s. It featured saxophonist Michael Stricklin, keyboardist Gary Walters, and guitarist Charlie Smith. They recorded one CD titled *Kindred Spirits* (1994).

Transportation

Group members include:

Anthony Cooper

Mark Cutsinger

Scott Davis

Eric Grimmet

Angie Walker

This Bloomington-based band emerged from the group The Beautiful Authentic Zoo Gods. Transportation seemed destined for stardom, but due to unexplained circumstances disbanded. Their one release was *Transportation*, recorded for Flat Earth Records in 1995.

Trinia & The Gypsies

Group members include:

Trinia Cox
Leta Essig
Catt Sadler
Jennifer Sparks

Indianapolis-native Trinia Cox's grandfathjer was an authentic Romanian gypsy. He and her violin-playing grandmother were both traditional with their song and dance. Trinia began playing piano at age eleven, and later switched to flute. She studied theatre and speech at Marian College in Indianapolis.

TRINA COX

Her first professional position was with the Jamaican Reggae band Quazar. Trinia sang and performed flute at popular nightspots such as the Vogue and The Patio. She graduated from Roosevelt University's Chicago School of Music with a Bachelor of Fine Arts degree in music. In 1991, she moved to Los Angeles and performed in television. After returning to Indianapolis in the early 1990s, she pursued a singing position with the group Rock Doll.

In 1996, Trinia formed the Gypsies (a high-octane show group) consisting of several singers and dancers. Their vocalizing and choreography filled the stage with excitement. Singer Catt Sadler of the Gypsies became became a television personality, actress/journalist and anchor for *E! News*. The Martinsville native also appeared in several movies and televisions shows.

THE GYPSIES
Left to right: Leta Essig, Jennifer Sparks and Catt Sadler

The Vulgar Boatmen

Group members include:

Erik Beaade
Dale Lawrence
Andy Richards
Matt Speak
(Robert Ray)

The Indianapolis-based group The Vulgar Boatmen descended from the band Right to Left. Formed by leader Dale Lawrence and Florida musician Robert Ray, this group was two bands with the same name. They performed in Indianapolis and the southern portion of the United States. They recorded three albums between 1989 and 1995 that received rave reviews in the United States and Europe. Two of their recordings include *You And Your Sister* (1989) on the Record Collect label, and *Please Panic* (1992) on Safehouse/Rough Trade.

Yun Hui

PHOTO CREDIT: LARRY GOSHEN

YUN HUI

Vocalist, keyboardist, performer and composer, Yun Hui was born in Kangwon Do, South Korea. She moved to the United States when she was seven. Raised in Columbus, she was classically trained on piano and violin. She became popular in the music business by promoting, producing and fronting her own band, Red Beans & Rice. She was video jockey for *Jazzbox,* a syndicated jazz television show, and developed a one-hour, all-original Hoosier artist radio program on WICR 88.7 in Indianapolis. Yun Hui is featured on *Red Bean & Rice, Staples* (1993), *Red Beans & Rice, Eat Big* (1996), *Red Beans & Rice, Yes We Can* (1999) and her debut as a single artist, *Yun Hui, Disoriental* (2000). Yun Hui lives in Hollywood, California, and is currently performing with guitarist Darren Stroud.

1990 Notables

Alligator Brothers
Amy Stephens
April Holbrook
Beki Brindle
Bernard Whittington
Beth Davis
Bigger Than Elvis
Bill Lancton
Blackbone
Boa
Brenda Williams
Carl Hines
Cathi Norton
Chooch & Enchanters
Chronic Reality
Corn Brothers
Dallas Miller
Dane Clark
Darin Patrick
Dave & Rae
Dead Mister Sunshine
Destination Earth
Direwolf
Fambooey
Fancy Lizards
Gordon Bonham
Greg Sansing
Gregg Bacon
Harvey & The Bluetones
Janiece Jaffe
JD & The 'Ol #7 Band
Jeff Deherdt
Jennifer Kirk
John Shaver

Joe Jackson
Johnny Socko
Kara Barnard
Keni Washington
Legendary Firebirds
Medicine Wheel
Michael Brown
Michael Kelsey
Mojo Hand
Monica Cantrell
Oliver Syndrome
Paul Holdman
Pure Gold
Radio Flyers
Rastabilly Rebels
Reggie Griffin
Rhett McDaniel
Rob Swayne
Rusty Bladen
Sam Gibson
Scott Greeson
Situation Grey
Suzanne Glass
The Blue Moon Boys
The Cooler Kings
The Kelly Jay Orchestra
The Mary Janes
The Remainders
The Shade
The Spirtles
The Why Store
Tony Medeiros
Yank Rachell

Country
& Western
Guys and Gals

Country & Western Guys and Gals

Country music mirrors the soul of Indiana like a good plate of grits. Those who love the sound of country crooners appreciate the music, since they believe the lyrics reflect the very essence of everyday life. Most importantly, they say, the listener can, unlike with other forms of modern music, actually understand the words.

Indiana's contribution to country music spreads a wide tablecloth. Famed entertainers such as Janie Fricke, Crystal Gayle, Sylvia and Steve Wariner are most prominent but artists such as Lattie Moore, Country Cousin Chickie, Charlie Gore, Charlie Stewart and Kim Crowley, all with ties to the Hoosier State, make their mark as well.

Television and radio stations flourished with country music in the 1950s. WIBC radio host Jack Morrow performed his morning *Country Carnival* program with guest artists Country Cousin Chickie and the Haymakers. Radio station WGEE, featuring disc jockey D.C. Mullins, was also popular.

WFBM television and radio produced such shows as *Indiana Hoedown,* featuring Charlie Gore, Herb and Kay, and the Swanee River Boys. Charlie Gore, a West Virginian and adopted Hoosier, lived in Indianapolis for many years. A former NBC network performer, Gore recorded for the famous King label.

Indiana Hoedown featured The Rangers. They provided background music for performers such as Lee Jones and Estil McNew's Jr. Kentucky Briarhoppers. The Rangers featured Walter Brown (accordion), Bob Boyer (bass), Ralph Cook (fiddle) and Charlie Gore (guitar).

Country stars picked their guitars and bowed their fiddles at such Indiana havens as the Sherman Bar, Blakes, the Thunderbird, Wagon Wheel and the Mocking Bird Hill. The White Cloud Jamboree in Greenwood was a must for country music buffs.

Locating information about Indiana-linked country musicians is a tall task, since so many have enjoyed brief success as entertainers. That doesn't deflect from the contribution they made to the country music scene. ***Country & Western Guys and Gals*** include:

The Angies – Wilson & Jones

THE ANGIES – WILSON & JONES

This popular singing duet from the Terre Haute area discovered their unique harmonies shortly after they became sister-in-laws. Inspired by the popular mother/daughter country duo The Judds, Angie Wilson and Angie Jones formed their own band and began performing at concerts, fairs and club circuits. They used their unique close-harmony blend of Southern rock and country to excite their audience throughout central and southern Indiana.

They won first place at the Little Nashville Opry's Country music contest, and since then have opened up for Ricky Van Shelton, Del Reeves and Whispering Bill Anderson. They continue to entertain in the Indiana area.

Jann Browne

Jann Browne was born in Anderson and raised in nearby Shelbyville. Her grandparents were members of the Kentucky Briarhoppers. They appeared regularly on the Grand Ole Opry. Meeting country stars inspired Jann, and she learned to play piano and sing at an early age. Browne made her first personal appearance in Shelbyville, performing at the local high school.

In 1978, she moved to California, wehre she spent two years performing with recording artists Asleep At The Wheel. In the 1990s, Browne released one album. It contained two singles, and both reached the Billboard charts. Recorded on the Curb label, "Tell Me Why" (1990) climbed to the #18 position and "Louisville" peaked at #75.

Aubrey Cagle

Aubrey Cagle was born in Lexington, Tennessee, but moved to Indianapolis around 1955. He purchased his first guitar at the age of eleven and performed with his own band at age seventeen. Cagle recorded "Real Cool" (1959), on the House Of Sounds label, and released "Be-Bop" and "Come Along Little Girl" (1960), both on Glee Records.

Cagle changed his name to Billy Love around 1961. He recorded several songs under that name. The recordings were on the Glee label. Although Cagle (Billy Love) never achieved national success, his friends in the music business included Carl Perkins, Elvis Presley and Ernest Tubb.

Left to right: Jerry Lee Williams, Jim Chenowith, Bryan Hightower, Aubrey Cagle, Jack Wagley and (Girl singer unknown) (1958).

Kim Cronley

Indianapolis native Kim Cronley began her professional singing career when she was fourteen. In the early 1980s, Cronley played many local nightspots including the Wreck Bar, Blake's, the Bonfire, Cowboys and Whiskey River. She sang and performed on the saxophone.

In 1988, Cronley was the opening act at the Little Nashville Opry in Nashville, Indiana, for Barbara Mandrell, George Jones, Tanya Tucker, Conway Twitty, Brenda Lee, Johnny Cash and many other country artists.

KIM CRONLEY

Jan Edwards

Singer Jan Edwards, a versatile performer, was born in Bloomington. Performing music with a range from Billie Holiday to Patsy Cline, she displayed her musical talent in many of Indiana's top clubs, including the Hilton, Radisson, Omni, the Vogue and the Broadmore Country Club. In 1970, Edwards was chosen Miss Indiana. She modeled and performed in many national and local commercials. After moving to Tennessee, Edwards performed at the Grand Ole Opry, and appeared with the Joe Edwards on the *Gitfiddle Review Show*.

JAN EDWARDS

Joe Edwards

Joe Edwards was born in Stanford, which is near Bloomington. He started his career in the early 1950s, performing on Bloomington's WTTV Channel 4, and WTTS radio. He appeared on *Uncle Bob Hardy's Hayloft Frolic* and the *Jack Noel's Happy Valley Show*. When Channel 4 moved to Indianapolis, Joe performed on television with artist Shorty Sheehan. Being an accomplished guitarist and fiddle player, he performed in 1955 at the Grand Ole Opry in Nashville. Edwards later performed with country artists Martha Carson, Bill Carlisle, Grandpa Jones, Jerry Reed, Little Jimmy Dickens and Wilma Lee & Stoney Cooper. In the late 1960s, he became a staff member of the Grand Ole Opry band. Edwards performed studio recording for labels such as Mercury, Columbia, Decca, Capitol and RCA. He worked with Chet Atkins and Owen Bradley, two of Nashville's greatest producers, and performed on national television with Dolly Parton and Tennessee Ernie Ford. His recording career includes performing with Ferlin Husky on his 1957 hit, "Gone," and backing such artists as Webb Pierce and Bobby Helms. Joe Edwards performed in the Nashville area, and was was featured in his own production, *The Gitfiddle Show*.

JOE EDWARDS

Buddy Emmons

Buddy Emmons was born on January 27, 1931 in Mishawaka, Indiana. He acquired his first steel guitar at age 11 and joined the Little Jimmy Dickens Band in Nashville at the age of 18. He recorded with many pop and country stars such as Ernest Tubb, Ray Price, Ray Charles and the Carpenters. Buddy Emmons died July 21, 2015.

BUDDY EMMONS

Tommy Flint

Tommy Flint was born Thomas Earl Flint in Dunmore, Kentucky. He moved to Indianapolis in 1954 and began playing his first guitar when he was 14. Flint played in the Indianapolis area for many years. He is well known as one of the greatest guitar thumb-pickers in country music. He performed in the Indianapolis area with such artists as rock-a-billy Lattie Moore, Bobby Helms and Joe Edwards. In the mid-1950s, Flint opened for Elvis Presley at the Lyric Theatre in Indianapolis. He also performed with such artists as Glen Campbell, Eddy Arnold, Ray Price, Merle Travis and Chet Atkins. Flint appeared on the Grand Ole Opry and the Country Music Hall of Fame and has won many awards for his great contribution to country music. Tommy has written and published over thirty books on instructional guitar for the Mel Bay Publications. Tommy Flint passed away in February of 2017 at the age of 82.

Left to right: Hardy Day, Tommy Flint, Jimmy Skinner and Curt Gibson (1955)

Left to right: Hardy Day, Tommy Flint, Lattie Moore and Curt Gibson (1955)

Janie Fricke

JANIE FRICKIE

Janie Fricke was born on December 19, 1947, in South Whitney. As a child, she was taught to play piano, organ and guitar. She performed at the local church. After graduating from Indiana University, Fricke moved to Memphis where she sang jingles and presented call letters for a local radio station. Around 1975, Janie sang backup for singers such as Tanya Tucker and Elvis Presley. In 1977, she recorded her first solo single, "What're You Doing Tonight," and five years later enjoyed her first big hit, "Don't Worry 'Bout Me, Baby." She later made many more hit recordings. In 1986, Fricke was named the most popular Female Solo Act by the International Country Music Awards. She is also a member of the Country Music Hall of Fame.

Crystal Gayle

Crystal Gayle (Brenda Gail Webb) was born January 9, 1951 in Paintsville, Kentucky. Her family moved to Wabash, Indiana when she was just a child. Early in her career, she performed with her two sisters, Loretta Lynn and Peggy Sue. At the age of sixteen, she toured with Loretta and Conway Twitty.

Gayle, confident she could enter the pop scene, left to pursue her own career. In 1973, she signed with United Artists Records. Gayle was chosen The Most Promising Country Female Vocalist of 1975. The album, *Must Believe In Magic* (1977) produced her biggest pop single ever, "Don't It Make My Brown Eyes Blue." Other hits were "I'll Get Over You" (1976) and "Ready For The Times To Get Better" (1978), both recorded on United Artists Records.

She is a member of the Grand Ole Opry and has a star on the Holllywood Walk of Fame.

CRYSTAL GAYLE

TIM GIBSON

Tim Gibson

Tim Gibson was born in Portsmouth, Ohio in 1958, and moved to Indiana at the age of four. He stared playing guitar at age nine and by the age of twelve was playing rock 'n'roll in his first band. He performed in the '70s with the bluegrass group First Annual Farewell Reunion, and has shared the stage with such artists as Jerry Reed, Bill Monroe, Jimmy Martin and Mac Wiseman. He now records, plays lead guitar and tours nationally with rockabilly legend Art Adams.

CHARLIE GORE

Charlie Gore

Charlie Gore was born in Chapmanville, West Virginia, and lived for many years in Indiana. He was a regular on *Indiana Hoedown* on WFBM radio and television in 1956. He recorded many records on the King label but his biggest hit was a rockabilly song in 1957 titled "Sock Hop" on the FAN Record label. Charlie Gore died June 30, 1984.

Haymakers

Group members include:

Paul Burton
Country Cousin Chickie (Chick Hopkins)
Tom Moriarty
Jack Simpson

This country & western band was formed in the mid-1950s. It featured fiddle, guitar, bass and accordion. A popular group in the Indianapolis area, the Haymakers performed regularly on WIBC Radio's *Jack Morrow's Hillbilly Hit Parade*.

HAYMAKERS

Jalene (Howse) Joyce

Deer Creek, Indiana, native Jalene Joyce started her music career in the early '50s with her two sisisters, Janet and Joetta, as The Three J's. They even had their own Saturday morning show on WSAL Radio in Logansport, Indiana. In 1958, Jalene traveled to the Orient and Europe with Uncle Bob Hardy & His Hayloft Frolic to entertain the troups. After returning from the Orient, she formed the all-girl band Jalene's Cowboys' Sweethearts and performed for two years at the Flame Café in Minneapolis, Minnesota. In 1960, under the name the Mello-Tones, she along with her husband Les Howse; her two sisters, Janet and Joetta; and musicians Karl Peterson and Bill Arledge she recorded one LP and two 45s. Jalene died October 3, 2019 at the age of 83.

JALENE (HOWSE) JOYCE

JALENE'S COWBOY'S SWEETHEARTS
Lynda, steel guitar; Patti, bass; Barbara Lee, guitar; and Jalene, accordion.

Sneaky Pete Kleinow

SNEAKY PETE KLEINOW

Peter E. Kleinow was born in South Bend, Indiana, on August 20, 1934. At the age of 17, he began to play the steel guitar. In 1965, while in Los Angeles, he took part in a recording sesson for The Ventures and began playing in local clubs. Two members of the Byrds, Cris Hillman and Gram Parsons, joined Kleinow's band and formed the Flying Burrito Brothers. The group's first album, *Guilded Palace of Sin,* has become a country-rock classic. The Burritos opened for the Rolling Stones and appeared in the film *Gimme Shelter.* Sneaky Pete Kleinow died of complications from Alzheimer's disease on January 6, 2017 at the age of 72.

Lattie Moore

Lattie Moore was not an Indiana native, but lived and performed in the Indianapolis area. Moore recorded his first song, "Juke Joint Johnny," on the Speed label in 1952. The record is a rare, and highly sought-after collector's item. It was later re-released in 1957 on the ARC Records label.

Moore played at several country bars in Indianapolis, and for a time operated the Thunderbird Nightclub. He spent most of his recording career on the famous King label and had several country hits in the 1960s. They included "Cajun Doll" and "Drunk Again." In 1961, the latter climbed to #25 in the top 100.

Lattie Moore died on June 13, 2010 at the age of 85.

Left to right: Spurs Ragsdale, Johnny Highland, Lattie Moore, Country Cousin Chickie, Patty Rindles, Bobby Phillips and Jackie Blair

LATTIE MOORE

Lenny Ray

LENNY RAY

Singer Lenny Ray, originally born in Manchester, Kentucky, moved to Indianapolis when he was twelve years old. In the mid 1950s, Lenny played the local country bars and performed in shows with artists such as Bill Monroe and Red Foley. He recorded two singles, "This Should Go On Forever"/"You Got Me Spinning" (1960s) and "No Man's Land"/"What Now?" (1970s), both on the Sweetwater label.

Running on Empty

RUNNING ON EMPTY (1982)
Left to right: Gary Brewer, Jackie Jacobsen, Gary Jacobsen and Kimmer Smith

Group members include:
Gary Brewer
Gary Jacobsen
Jackie Jacobsen
Kimmer Smith

This country/rock band was formed around 1982 in Indianapolis. They performed in the local bar scene. Drummer Gary Brewer later performed at the Little Opry in Nashville, Indiana, and opened for many national country artists. Guitarist Kimmer Smith and bassist Gary Jacobsen perform in the Indiana area. They appeared with such artists as Dolly Parton. This group also featured Jackie Jacobsen, one of Indiana's top female bass players. Jackie passed away on July 2, 2013, and drummer Gary Brewer died on July 27, 2017 at the age of 63.

Shorty Sergent

In 1958, Rock-a-billy singer Shorty Sergeant recorded a popular local hit titled "Record Hop," on the Jet Records label. Shorty was quite popular on the country and western circuit and performed on the Indianapolis bar scene.

Left to right: Bobby Ridenour and Shorty Sergent

Connie Smith

Connie Smith was born in Elkhart. She won her first amateur talent contest in the early 1960s Guitarist Chet Atkins heard her sing and convinced Bill Anderson to write a song for her titled, "Once A Day." It became Connie's biggest hit and was voted Song of the Year in 1964. She then reached stardom by recording such songs as "Ain't Had No Lovin'," "The Hurtin's All Over," "Baby's Back Again," "Then And Only Then," "If I Talk To Him" and "(Till) I Kissed You." In 1971, she joined the Grand Ole Opry. In 1992, Smith was inducted into the Country Music Hall of Fame.

Sylvia

(Sylvia Kirby Allen)

Sylvia was born in Kokomo on December 9, 1956. Her dreams of becoming a country singer began early in her childhood. After graduating from high school, she moved to Nashville, Tennessee. Sylvia recorded the song, "You Don't Miss A Thing" in 1979. It was a Billboard top 40 hit. In 1980, Sylvia recorded "Tumbleweed," a top 10 hit with RCA. Sylvia's greatest success was "Drifter" (1981). It occupied the #1 position for one week on the Billboard charts. Sylvia recorded many other songs, and later collaborated with several songwriters. She co-wrote songs for artists such as the Statler Brothers and Jimmy Fortune.

CIRCLE B RANCH GANG
Left to right: Country Cousin Chickie (Hopkins), Paul Burton, Tom Moriarty, Ann Wagner, Dick Pittenger and Dick Green

Ann Wagner

Born in Louisville, Kentucky, Ann Wagner was raised in Vincennes. She began on the piano and violin in grade school and studied voice while attending the Saint Rose Academy. She began her broadcasting career in WAOV Radio in Vincennes. After moving to Indianapolis, she performed nights at the Columbia Club, and days on *PM Party* at WIBC.

In the early 1950s, Wagner was a country singer for WFBM Television's *Circle B Ranch* program. At that time WFBM featured both radio and television. Wagner became the first female disc jockey in Indiana.

In 1961, at the age of thirty-seven, she attended Butler University and received her master's degree. She became assistant professor for the radio and television department at Butler University in Indianapolis. In 1988, after twenty years in broadcasting, she retired from Butler University.

Steve Wariner

Steve Wariner was born in Noblesville on Christmas Day in 1954. He became a successful country artist by playing bass with country stars Bob Luman and Chet Atkins. In 1971, Wariner became the bass player with the Dottie West band and remained with her until 1974. He signed with RCA in 1978, and climbed the charts with, "All Roads Lead To You" (1981).

Steve later switched to the MCA label and continued success with "Some Fools Never Learn" (1985), "Life's Highway" (1986), and "Lynda" (1987).

Billed as a singer/songwriter, Steve Wariner continues to be a hot attraction on the country & western circuit.

STEVE WARINER

SONNY GRUBBS & THE HOOSIER ALL-STARS (1950s)

Sonny Grubbs is pictured top middle. Photograph taken at the All Stars Jamboree in the Lyric Theatre, Indianapolis.

The Jazzmakers

The Jazzmakers

*I*ndiana jazz musicians deserve a book of their own. Throughout the twentieth century they contributed to the evolution of a type of music that embodies the very spirit of the music scene. New Orleans-bred artists such as Louis Armstrong, Al Hirt and Sidney Bechet may have birthed the sound, but Indiana artists created musical tones that enhanced the popularity of jazz.

If Indiana were to have a Jazz Hall of Fame, the collection of artists would be never-ending. Among those who captured the hearts of jazz lovers everywhere were Wes, Monk, and Buddy Montgomery, Freddie Hubbard, Hoagy Carmichael, Slide Hampton, J.J. Johnson, and David Baker. Others such as Steve Allee, Royce Campbell, Jimmy Coe, and Alonzo "Pookie" Johnson were outstanding.

Jazz clubs were an integral part of the Indiana music arena. In the 1950s, The Sunset Terrace, The British Lounge, the 440 Club, Henri's and George's Bar flourished. Jazz musicians from around the world played at those venues and at the Pink Poodle, the Missile Club, and the Barrington Lounge.

Jazz outlets spilling out the dynamic tones of jazz include the Jazz Kitchen, owned by jazz musician David Allee. That club and proprietor David Andrichik's Chatterbox feature Indiana jazz artists and noted musicians with national and international reputations.

Jazzmakers that have shined wherever they have performed include:

Affinity

AFFINITY (1989)
Left to right: Larry King, Art Reiner and Kevin Kaiser, with Royce Campbell in front.

This jazz/fusion group was formed in 1976. It featured original members Royce Campbell, Terry Cook, Larry King, Art Reiner and Bruce Stanforth. A later member was percussionist Kevin Kaiser. Affinity recorded one album, *Around The Town* (1987), on the Raised Eyebrow label. Member Larry King passed away on March 4, 2018 at the age of 64.

David Allee

David Allee was born March 24, 1969 in Indianapolis. The son of noted jazz pianist Steve Allee and proprietor of the popular Jazz Kitchen, David has been an accomplished trumpet player for more than twenty years. He performs on stage with many groups and continues to operate one of the top jazz clubs in the United States.

PHOTO CREDIT: LARRY GOSHEN

DAVID ALLEE

Steve Allee

Indianapolis-born Steve Allee served in the 82nd Airborne Division Army Band. After a short stint with the Buddy Rich band, Steve returned to Indiana to pursue his jazz career. As a pianist and composer, he co-led the Von Ohlen-Allee Big Band with drummer John Von Ohlen. He performed at many jazz festivals, including the Montreux Jazz Festival in Switzerland. Steve has written and arranged recordings for television sound tracks including *The Lost World*, NBC's *Name Your Adventure* and ABC's *America's Best Kept Secrets*. His recording credits were featured on the syndicated *Bob and Tom Show* as well as the recordings of other artists. Recordings under his own name include *The Magic Hour* (1995) on Noworthy Records, *Mirage*, (2003) *New York in the Fifties* (2001), on the AlleeOlp label. In 2006, he signed with the Indianapolis Jazz label Owl Studios and released *Colors*, (2007) and *Dragonfly* in 2008. As of 2018, Steve Allee continues to be active in the field of Jazz.

STEVE ALLEE

Kevin Anker

Indiana born Kevin Anker began playing piano at the age of four, and in high school performed in garage bands playing classic rock 'n' roll. He plays a wide range of music, from blues to rock n' roll and jazz. Anker can be heard on many recordings from Tad Robinson and Cynthia Layne, as well as many others. As and author, he published a book on keyboard sounds titled *Live Sounds for Keyboard*. As of this writing, Kevin Anker is performing and toruing with The Fabulous Thunder Birds.

PHOTO CREDIT: LARRY GOSHEN

KEVIN ANKER

David Baker

David Baker was born on December 21, 1931 in Indianapolis. Early in his career, he performed with jazz legends Wes Montgomery and Slide Hampton. David toured on trombone with Buddy Johnson and in 1956 performed with the Stan Kenton Orchestra. In 1957, he worked with Maynard Ferguson, and in 1961 joined the Lionel Hampton band. After a stint with Quincy Jones in 1962, a muscular disease forced Baker to concentrate on the cello. David Baker was President of the International Association for Jazz Education and Professor/Chairman of Jazz Studies at Indiana University. A musician, composer and educator, David Baker passed away on March 26, 2016 at the age of 86.

PHOTO CREDIT: LARRY GOSHEN

DAVID BAKER

Benny Barth

PHOTO CREDIT: LARRY GOSHEN

Left to right: Benny Barth and Frank Glover (1988)

Benny Barth was born on February 16, 1929 in Indianapolis. He studied tap dancing at the age of four and played the accordion and trumpet in grade school. While attending Shortridge High School, he played drums with the Barton Rogers Orchestra. Benny performed on the infamous Indiana Avenue at such nightspots as Andres, George's Bar and the Cotton Club. He performed locally with Erroll Grandy, Buddy Parker, Slide Hampton, Leroy Vinnegar, David Baker, Jimmy Coe and Freddie Hubbard. Barth was also a regular member of the Buddy and Monk Montgomery group, The Mastersounds. Barth recorded thirteen albums for the World Pacific label and two for Fantasy Records. He has two recordings on the Fantasy label with Vince Guaraldi, including the original sound track of *A Boy Named Charlie Brown*. For three years, Barth was the house drummer at the popular Hungri I in San Francisco. He performed with such artists as Barbara Streisand, Mel Tormé and Jon Hendricks. Other musicians Benny recorded with include Joe Venuti, Ben Webster, Jimmy Witherspoon, Pearl Bailey and Joe Williams. Benny Barth passed away on January 27, 2017 at the age of 86.

John Bunch

John Bunch was born in 1921 in Tipton. He began playing piano at the age of eleven, but never played professionally until his mid-thirties. In the early 1950s, Bunch performed with Georgie Auld, and in the late 1950s played with Woody Herman, Benny Goodman and Maynard Ferguson. From 1966 through 1972, Bunch was musical director for Tony Bennett. He also performed and directed the Buddy Rich band. As the leader of his own band (1975-1977), he recorded five albums under his name.

Gary Burton

GARY BURTON

Anderson native Gary Burton studied piano at age six. He was self-taught on the vibes. In 1963, he toured the United States and Japan with pianist George Shearing. In 1964, he joined the Stan Getz quartet. They performed at the White House. Burton also appeared in two films, *The Hanged Man* and *Get Yourself A College Girl*.

In the late 1960s, he formed his own group with guitarist Larry Coryell. Since 1970 he frequently performed with Keith Jarrett and Chick Corea. On June of 2017, the Seven-time Grammy Winner Gary Burton announced his retirement from touring at the age of 74.

GARY BURTON TRIO (1955)

Candoli Brothers

The Candoli Brothers, Pete and Conte, were born in Mishawaka in the 1920s. Pete performed on trumpet with top name bands such as Tommy Dorsey, Glen Miller, Woody Herman, Stan Kenton, and Count Basie. He composed and arranged music for Judy Garland, Ella Fitzgerald, and Peggy Lee. He also recorded with Henry Mancini, Nelson Riddle and Quincy Jones.

Brother Conte joined the Woody Herman Band in 1945 and remained a permanent member for ten years. He also performed with Benny Goodman, Dizzy Gillespie and Stan Kenton. In 1954, he formed his own group with sidemen Chubby Jackson, Frank Rosolino and Lou Levy. Conte moved to Los Angeles and for four years joined the Lighthouse All-Stars featuring Shorty Rogers, Bud Shank and Bob Cooper. He recorded with Gerry Mulligan, Shelly Manne, Terry Gibbs, Frank Sinatra, Bing Crosby, Sammy Davis Jr. and Sarah Vaughn. In 1967, Conte joined the *Tonight Show* starring Johnny Carson. He became a permanent member of the Doc Severinsen Orchestra and remained with Severinsen until Carson's retirement in 1992.

The Candoli Brothers have performed and appeared on television and in movies. Conte died December 14, 2001, and Pete passed away on January 11, 2008. Both died from prostate cancer.

ROYCE CAMPBELL

Royce Campbell

Since his stepfather was a naval office, Royce Campbell, a native of Seymour, Indiana, was raised in Japan, Spain, Barbados, Pennsylvania and South Carolina. Learning to play the guitar at the age of nine, he was first influenced by blues, rock and then jazz. After graduating from high school, Campbell moved to Indianapolis to live with his uncle, musician Carroll DeCamp. Campbell later toured with Marvin Gaye, and in 1975 began a long stint with the Henry Mancini Orchestra. Royce has performed with Richard "Groove" Holmes, Jack McDuff, Sarah Vaughn, Nancy Wilson, Melvin Rhyne and Joe Williams. He has recorded more than ten albums under his own name. He lives in Harrisburg, Virginia, and continues to be a successful recording artist.

Hoagy Carmichael

Born November 11, 1899 in Bloomington, Hoagy Carmichael wrote his most popular composition "Stardust" in 1929. He composed many other great songs until his death in 1981. Active in the 1950s, Carmichael played a cameo roll in the film, *A Man With A Horn,* a moved based on the life of Bix Beiderbecke. In 1951, he won an Academy Award for his composition, "In The Cool, Cool, Cool Of The Evening." He also recorded several albums, one with jazz legends Art Pepper and Jimmy Rowles in the 1950s. In the early '60s, Carmichael toured the United States and Europe, making solo appearances and performing on radio and television. Hoagy Carmichael provided many great compositions including "Up The Lazy River," "Skylark," and "Georgia On My Mind."

PHOTO CREDIT: DUNCAN SCHIEDT

HOAGY CARMICHAEL

Chuck Carter

An Illinois native, Chuck Carter established his home in Indianapolis in the early sixties. He joined the Stan Kenton Orchestra in 1971 as a baritone saxophone soloist. With Kenton, he toured the United States and several European countries and performed in several of Kenton's recordings. In 1974, he formed an 18-piece band that included John Von Ohlen and Steve Allee. He worked in various groups around Indianapolis, including the Carter/Markiewiez Jazz Quartet. As a member of the Indianapolis Jazz Foundation Hall of Fame, Chuck Carter continued to perform until his death in 2003.

STAN KENTON ORCHESTRA

Three Indiana musicians, Chuck Carter, Ramon Lopez and Dick Schearer with Stan Kenton.

Marvin Chandler

Born in Bloomington, Indiana, Reverend Marvin Chandler received his bachelor's degree from Indiana University and served as a pastor of Bloomington's Second Baptist Church. As an accomplished jazz pianist, he has performed with some of Indiana's top jazz icons, and in 2003 was inducted into the Indianapolis Jazz Foundation Hall of Fame. In 2019 he was a recipient of the Ralph Adams Lifetime Achievement Award, and today continues to perform in Indiana's top jazz clubs and concerts.

PHOTO CREDIT: LARRY GOSHEN

MARVIN CHANDLER AND MINGO JONES

Lawrence Clark III

Lawrence Clark III grew up in Indianapolis. His family was musically inclined and he became a percussionist. He performed with some of the world's finest musicians, including Grover Washington, Richard Groove Holmes, David "Fathead" Newman, and James Moody. He also played with jazz legends Jimmy Coe, Erroll Grandy, Pookie Johnson and David Young. Clark is a teacher of percussion and jazz and continues to educate and influence the young artists of today.

PHOTO CREDIT: LARRY GOSHEN

LAWRENCE CLARK III

Jimmy Coe

Jimmy Coe was born in Tompkinsville, Kentucky, but he has lived in Indianapolis since the late 1930s. From 1950 until 1953, Jimmy performed with his own band at the Cotton Club on Indiana Avenue. In 1953, he recorded the R&B hit, "After Hours Joint," on the State label. Coe also recorded for the King label in Cincinnati under the name of Jimmy Cole.

Left to right: Jimmy Coe and Erroll Grandy (1988)

In the 1960s, Coe performed with the trio that included Melvin Rhyne on B-3 organ and drummer Sonny Johnson. This trio entertained at clubs such as the Barrington Lounge and the Pink Poodle. Coe performed with some of the greatest jazz legends including Freddie Hubbard, J.J. Johnson, Jay McShann, Tiny Bradshaw and many others. He is well known for his "big band" sounds.

In 1994, he recorded his CD, *Say What?*, on Time Records. That recording was dedicated to Jimmy Munford, who was Coe's drummer since 1970; and William "Whitey" Harris, whose last recording was that CD. Jimmy continued to perform in the Indianapolis area, playing special engagements and working in top clubs. He died on Feburary 28, 2004 at the age of 82.

Cal Collins

Born in Medora, Indiana, Cal Collins grew up listening to country and western music. While playing guitar at the age of thirteen, he was influenced by the form of jazz. In the 1950s, he performed in a local jazz quartet. After spending two years in the Army, he settled in Cincinnati. Cal spent three years touring with the famous Benny Goodman band, performing in concerts across the USA and in Europe and Japan.

Eddie Condon

Eddie Condon was born in Goodland, Indiana. He became a professional jazz banjoist at the age of seventeen. Condon performed with such artists as Jimmy McParland, Bud Freeman and Red Nichols. He recorded with such jazz greats as Louis Armstrong, Jack Teagarden and Gene Kruppa. In the 1950s, Eddie recorded on the Columbia label, and in 1957 toured Great Britain with his own group. In 1964, he toured Australia and New Zealand. He was able to attend his own benefit concert at Carnegie Hall shortly before his death in 1973.

David Darling

David Darling was born in Elkhart on March 4, 1941. He studied piano at the age of four and began to play the cello at age ten. He played bass and alto sax in high school and studied classical cello at Indiana University. David worked with the Paul Winter Consort from 1970 through 1978, and toured throughout the USA while recording four albums. He recorded several other albums including Ralph Towner's *Old Friends, New Friends* (1979), with Kenny Wheeler, Michael DiPasqua and Eddie Gomez. Darling recorded in 1980 with vibraharpist Dave Samuels. In 1981, he was co-founder of a group named Gallery. That group successfully recorded and toured throughout the USA. Darling plays both traditional cello and his self-designed eight-string solid-body. By using such attachments as an echoplex, ring modulator and a fuzz box, he plays a variety of music from traditional classic to rock and jazz.

DICK DICKSON

Dick Dickinson

Drummer Dick Dickinson was born on January 2, 1928 in Emory, Georgia. He was raised in Petersburg, Indiana. Dick played with the George Boldi Dance Orchestra from 1950 through 1951. In 1952, he performed with the Freddy Dale Orchestra. They placed second in Indiana University's National College Jazz Competition. In the mid-1950s, Dick played the local jazz clubs and performed with such artists as David Baker, Al Kiger and Jimmy Coe. From 1970 until 1972, he was producer and host for *Explorations in Jazz*, a radio show on WFIU at Indiana University. His radio show *Just Jazz*, was aired on WIAN from 1985 until 1986 and on WFYI Radio from 1986 until 1990. In 1985, Dick was awarded the Key to the City of Indianapolis and was later inducted into the Jazz Foundation Hall of Fame. Dickinson passed away in December of 2008 at the age of 80.

Rob Dixon

A Native of Alanta, Georgia, Rob Dixon attended Indiana University. He was influenced in jazz by renowned educator David Baker. He moved to New York in 1998 and worked with the Illinois Jacquet's Big Band. Dixon returned to Indianapolis in 2003 to work with the Buselli-Wallarb Jazz Orchestra and lead his own funk group "Triology+1" with organist Melvin Rhyne.

PHOTO CREDIT: LARRY GOSHEN

ROB DIXON

Frank Glover

Frank Glover was born June 27, 1963 in Indianapolis. He attended Indiana University School of Music. His specialty is the clarinet and saxophone. Glover performed regularly at the popular Chatterbox jazz club and appeared weekly at The Jazz Kitchen. Glover produced five CDs under his own name, *Mosaic* (1991), *Something Old, Something New* (1994), and the clarinet/piano duo with Claude Sifferlen, *Siamese Twins,* (1999) on FGA Records. *Politico* (2009) and *Abacus* (2010) on the Owl label. He performed at Carnegie Hall in 1996, and also played the Chicago Jazz Festival. Frank won the 1995 National Endowment for the Arts Jazz Performance award.

PHOTO CREDIT: LARRY GOSHEN

FRANK GLOVER

Erroll Grandy

Erroll Grandy (known to his friends as "Groundhog"), was born on January 2, 1921 in Norfolk, Virginia. Erroll moved to Indianapolis in 1936. He graduated from Crispus Attucks High School. In 1942, Grandy attended Jordan's Conservatory of Music. He was partially blind, but that was no handicap. Grandy was well-known in Indianapolis as the Godfather of Jazz. He was considered a mentor to many local jazz musicians such as Wes Montgomery, Freddie Hubbard, Slide Hampton and J.J. Johnson. In the early 1950s, Grandy formed his own group and performed at clubs such as the Ritz Lounge and Henri's Petri Room on fabled Indiana Avenue. In 1953, he performed with the Jimmy Coe Band, and in 1955 joined the Count Fisher Trio. Erroll Grandy died on June 12, 1991.

PHOTO CREDIT: LARRY GOSHEN

EVERETTE GREENE (1998)

Everett Greene

Born in Washington, D.C., Greene moved to Indiana in the early 1950s. A long-time resident of Indianapolis, he started his musical career as a gospel singer. Now singing pop/jazz, he has performed at the popular Jazz Kitchen, ChatterBox and other points across the city. He performed many years with the Jimmy Coe Band and can be heard on his own recordings and as guest singer on the recordings of others.

Rayford Griffin

Rayford Griffin was born February 6, 1958 in Indianapolis. He studied drums at age thirteen. While attending Shortridge High School, he performed with a band called Tarnished Silver. That group included singer/guitarist Kenny Edmonds, better known today as Babyface. After graduating high school, Rayford joined the band Merging Traffic. This group opened for many big name

RAYFORD GRIFFIN

acts, including Grover Washington and Jean-Luc Ponty. In 1980, while opening for Ponty, Griffin had the chance to tour and record with the Jean-Luc Ponty band. He recorded six albums with Jean-Luc Ponty including *Mystical Adventures* (1982), *Individual Choice* (1983), *Open Mind* (1984) and *Fables* (1985) all on the Atlantic label. *The Gift Of Time* (1987) and *Storytelling* (1989) on CBS Records.

Griffin has recorded with Boyz II Men, George Howard, Stanley Clarke, George Duke and Patrice Rushen, among others. He has toured and performed with Michael Jackson, Anita Baker, The Isley Brothers, Bette Midler, Babyface, Manhattan Transfer and Cameo. A writer/singer and a drummer, he lives in California and released his own CD in 2002 titled *Rebirth Of The Cool*.

Slide Hampton

Slide (Locksley) Hampton was born in Jennette, Pennsylvania, but he and his musical family moved to Indianapolis in the early 1940s. Hampton performed with Buddy Johnson in the 1950s. Between 1955 and '56, he performed with the Lionel Hampton Band. In 1957, Slide played trombone and arranged for Maynard Ferguson. From 1959 through 1962, he was musical arranger for singer Lloyd Price. Six years later, Hampton performed and toured Europe with the Woody Herman Band.

In 1977, he formed his own group, The World of Trombones. Hampton is responsible for many recordings including *Sister Salvation* (1960), *Jazz with A Twist* (1962), and *Two Sides Of Slide* (1962).

PHOTO CREDIT: LARRY GOSHEN

SLIDE HAMPTON

Cherryl Hayes

Cherryl Hayes was born in Indianapolis and graduated from Crispus Attucks High School. She performed locally at the Jazz Kitchen and the Indy Jazz Fest. She was voted Best Indy Jazz Vocalist by *Nuvo Weekly Magazine*. Cherryl appeared internationally at the Oriental Hotel in Bangkok, Thailand, and performed for the King and Queen of Bangkok. She was featured at the Tavern on the Green in New York City, and perfomed for President Barak Obama on November 18, 2002. Hayes continues to perform locally and nationally.

Dave Hepler

PHOTO CREDIT: LARRY GOSHEN

DAVE HELPER

Indiana native Dave Hepler took his first piano lesson at the age of eight. He studied trumpet at age nine, and was playing professionally in his father's band by the time he was eleven. Dave studied music at Indiana University. While living with his trumpet-playing father, he turned his main interest to jazz. Dave resides in the Indianapolis area and has performed at such clubs as the Stillwater, Chatterbox, the City Taproom, and the Midtown Café. One of his earlier trios consisted of Jay Hammel on guitar and Harold Cardwell on drums. Dave's recordings include *Anomaly, Birthday Wish* (1994) and *Dave Hepler 4* (2001), featuring Matt Thompson on bass.

Carl Hines

Born in Wilson, North Carolina, Hines played music throughout his life, but chose a career as a math teacher. He taught for thirty-five years in the Indianapolis area.

As a part time pianist, he performed with many of the Indiana Avenue jazz legends. He formed the Carl Hines Band and continues to perform as a single/group pianist.

PHOTO CREDIT: LARRY GOSHEN

CARL HINES

Freddie Hubbard

Indianapolis-born Freddie Hubbard enjoyed his first professional engagement with two of Indiana's top jazz icons, Wes and Monk Montgomery. After moving to New York in the late 1950s, he performed with saxophonist Sonny Rollins, Slide Hampton, J.J. Johnson and Quincy Jones. In 1961, Hubbard played a long stint with the Art Blakey's Jazz Messengers. He won the DownBeat New Star Award for trumpet. Between 1966 an 1970, Hubbard recorded a series of his own albums on the Atlantic label. He recorded with some of the world's top jazz musicians including Oliver Nelson, Eric Dolphy, Herbie Hancock, Wayne Shorter and Max Roach. Freddie is responsible for successful recordings on Blue Note and other labels. Freddie Hubbard passed away on December 29, 2008 at the age of 70.

PHOTO CREDIT: DUNCAN SCHIEDT

FREDDIE HUBBARD

Bill Jennings

Bill Jennings

BILL JENNINGS

Born in Indianapolis, left-handed guitar player Jennings played guitar upside down. He has recorded with Jack McDuff, King Curtis, Louis Armstrong, Bill Doggett and Louis Jordan. Because of his wide range of musical knowledge, Jennings can be found on recordings from bebop to pop. Some of his recordings under his name were "Three Little Words" and "Day Train" on the King Records label and his LP, *The Fabulous Guitar of Bill Jennings*. Later in his career he lost a finger on his fretting hand and began to play the electric bass. Bill Jennings died in 1978 at the age of 59.

Janiece Jaffe

PHOTO CREDIT: LARRY GOSHEN

JANIECE JAFFE

Janiece grew up in Bloomington, Indiana, in a musical family. Her mother was an opera singer and her father a professor of classical music. As a singer, she performed with Freddie Hubbard, Al Cobine, Monika Herzig and many others. Janiece Jaffe has recorded 11 albums and can be heard on more then 25 other recordings as a guest vocalist. She has received her B.A. in Vocal Jazz Performance from Indiana University, and continues to entertain in the Indiana area.

Alonzo "Pookie" Johnson

Alonzo "Pookie" Johnson was born in 1927 in Indianapolis. He attended Crispus Attucks High School and Butler University's Arthur Jordan College of Music. After leaving the U.S. Army Air Force, Johnson traveled with many bands including the Eddie Bird Sextet, Sax Kare Band, King Kolax Big Band, the Montgomery-Johnson Quintet and the Jimmy Coe Orchestra. He performed on Indiana Avenue at some of the most legendary jazz clubs including the Walker Casino, the Sunset Terrace, the British Lounge, the 440 Club, Henri's, and George's Bar. Johnson performed with Wes, Monk and Buddy Montgomery, Willis Kirk, Freddie Hubbard, Slide Hampton, Leroy Vinnegar, Jimmy Coe, Russell Webster, The Hampton Sisters, and many others. His discography includes Buddy Montgomery's *Montgomery Brothers and Five Others,* Russell Webster's *Together Again,* Jimmy Coe's *Say What* and the compilation album *Almost Forgotten Artists* on Columbia Records. Alonzo "Pookie" Johnson died on September 3, 2005 at the age of 77.

ALONZO "POOKIE" JOHNSON

J.J. Johnson

J.J. Johnson was born January 22, 1924 in Indianapolis. In 1942, at the age of eighteen, he joined the Benny Carter band. He later performed with the Count Basie Orchestra. In 1946, Johnson recorded in New York under his own name with Esquire All Stars. He later performed with such big name artists as Illinois Jacquet, Dizzy Gillespie, and Oscar Pittiford. In 1954, Johnson co-led a quintet with trombonist Kai Winding that toured Europe and made several memorable recordings. From 1956 through 1960, he played with his own group. In 1961, he toured with the legendary Miles Davis. As a writer, Johnson scored many compositions. In 1970, he moved to Los Angeles to pen sound tracks for movies and television. J.J. Johnson recorded, *Jay Jay Johnson All Stars* (1953), *Blue Trombone* (1959), and *A Touch Of Satin* (1962). After a short retirement in the late 1990s, Johnson passed away on February 4, 2001 at the age of 77. He will be remembered as one of the world's greatest jazz trombonists.

PHOTO CREDIT: DUNCAN SCHIEDT

J.J. JOHNSON

Mingo Jones

PHOTO CREDIT: LARRY GOSHEN

MINGO JONES

Mingo Jones was born December 12, 1928 in Saint Joseph, Missouri. After being stationed with the 35th U.S. Army Band at Fort Harrison in Indiana, Mingo made Indianapolis his home. In the early 1950s, Mingo had the chance to play bass for guitarist Wes Montgomery. He later became one of the top bass players of the famous Indiana Avenue scene. Jones performed with some of Indiana's top musicians, including Pookie Johnson, Jimmy Coe, Erroll Grandy, Marvin Chandler, Melvin Rhyne, David Baker, Freddie Hubbard, Slide Hampton, Everett Greene, and many others.

While playing a long stint at the Embers Show Lounge in Indianapolis, Mingo had the opportunity to back up national acts including Barbara McNair, Helen O'Connel, Bobby Short and Mel Tormé.

Mingo Jones died of throat cancer on April 3, 2017 at the age of 89.

Larry Leggett

Larry Leggett was born on October 23, 1921 in Brazil, Indiana. He was the youngest member of the Brazil marching band. From 1948 to 1978, he taught music at Crispus Attucks High School in Indianapolis. He maintained a great reputation as a saxophone player who could have easily hit the road with the band of his choice. From 1950 to 1956 Leggett performed with Three Flips and a Flop, a combo that played the night club circuit in Indiana. The Larry Liggett Band played a regular gig at the Marriott and Stoufers for several years. He recorded a live album at the Stouffer's Inn and recorded several singles for the Chess Record label. Larry Leggett died January 29, 2001 at the age of 79.

Harry Miedema

Saxophonist Harry Miedema began his career by playing for the Lawrence Central high School band in Indianapolis. In the early 1970s, Miedema attended Indiana University School of Music and studied under jazz icon David Baker. Miedema was music director for the O'jays for 22 years, and has performed with such artists as Lou Rawls, Natalie Cole and the Temptations. Television performances include *The Today Show, Oprah Winfrey* and the Quincy Jones show, *Vibe*.

Buddy Montgomery & Monk Montgomery

Wes Montgomery may have garnered most of the headlines with his talents on the guitar, but brothers Monk and Buddy left their mark on the jazz landscape as well. In 1952, Monk, while performing with the Lionel Hampton band, made musical history by becoming the first jazz musician to play the Fender electric bass. He continued to perform around the world with famed musicians who enjoyed his unique style. Monk is credited with creating the Las Vegas Jazz Society.

Buddy Montgomery was the music arranger for the brothers. His favored musical instrument was the piano, but in 1957 he won the DownBeat Award for New Star of the Year on the vibraphone. He also won the New Jazz Arranger of the Year award.

He and Monk organized the Mastersounds, a quartet that was quite popular. Buddy Montgomery's CD, *Buddy Montgomery, Live at Maybeck Recital Hall,* is considered a classic.

Monk died on May 20, 1982, and Buddy passed away on May 14, 2009.

Wes Montgomery

Born in Indianapolis, Indiana, on March 6, 1925, Wes was a self-taught guitarist whose original style and the use of octaves changed the form of guitar playing. After learning to play the instrument in his teenage years and playing in local clubs, Wes was discovered by Lionel Hampton. He toured with the Hampton's band in 1948. In the 1950s, he returned to Indianapolis to perform in some of the top jazz clubs. In 1957 and '58 he recorded with the Mastersounds, a group formed by his brothers Monk and Buddy Montgomery. They recorded several albums.

In 1959, Wes recorded with his own trio, featuring organist Melvin Rhyne. In 1960, Wes performed briefly with the John Coltrane Sextet in San Francisco, and later recorded with the Wynton Kelly Trio. In the mid-1960s, he achieved international notoriety with his instrumental pop recordings, "Goin' Out Of My Head" and "California Dreaming." In 1967 he made an appearance on television with Herb Alpert.

Wes died of a heart attack on June 15, 1968.

Mary Ann Moss

JOHN VON OHLEN QUARTET (1972)
*Left to right: John Von Ohlen, Mary Ann Moss,
Claude Sifferlen and Steve Allee*

Indianapolis singer Mary Ann Moss started her music career by singing with pianist Jimmy McDaniels. She has performed in clubs and given concerts across the world, from St. Louis to Japan. Mary worked with the Al Cobine Band and the John Von Ohlen Quartet that featured Steve Allee and Claude Sifferlen. Retired from music, she now spends her time as a skilled painter.

Left to right: Wes Montgomery, Monk Montgomery and Buddy Montgomery.

Tom Mullinix

THE JESTONES
Left to right: Tommy Mullinix, Savannah Churthill, Morry Wide and Jerry North

A native of Indianapolis, Tom Mullinix was a nationally known band leader, trumpet player and vocalist. He played Dixieland style, which is the music he loved. Mullinix performed with many different bands, including the Naptown Strutters. In the 1980s, he opened his own jazz club, The Jazz Celler, in Indianapolis at Union Station. Tom Mullinix died on December 28, 2010.

Bill Myers

PHOTO CREDIT: LARRY GOSHEN

BILL MYERS

Indianapolis born Bill Myers is a professional actor, film and TV producer, and Jazz musician. He attended Broad Ripple High School and became interested in music at an early age. While playing bass, he has performed wth some of Indiana's greatist jazz musicians such as Jimmy Coe, Pookie Johnson, Melvin Rhyne, and many others. Bill Myers continues to perform, produce and live in the Indianapolis area.

Myriad

Group members include:

Royce Campbell
Terry Cook
Larry King
Art Reiner
Bruce Stanforth

This jazz/fusion group was formed in the mid-1970s. It was the forerunner of the band Affinity.

MYRIAD (1976)
Left to right: Bruce Stanforth, Larry King, Terry Cook, Royce Campbell and Art Reiner

Oliver Nelson, Jr.

Oliver Nelson Jr. was born in St. Louis, Missouri. He moved to Indianapolis in 1979. The son of famous jazz artist, Oliver Nelson Sr., he received his master's of music performance degree on flute from Butler University in Indianapolis. Nelson has performed with his father and recorded with Benny Golson, Bob Crenshaw, David Baker and drummer Grady Tate. In 1996, his band won the WTPI Jazz Festival Competition. He continues to lead his own band and perform at some of the top jazz clubs in Indianapolis.

PHOTO CREDIT: LARRY GOSHEN

OLIVER NELSON, JR.

JOHN VON OHLEN

Von Ohlen performed with, among others, Billy Maxted, Woody Herman and Stan Kenton.
He died on October 3, 2018.

Paula Owen

Singer Paula Owen was born in Columbus, Ohio. She has lived in Muncie for several years. Owen performed with the Trotty Heck Quartet at Rick's Café in downtown Indianapolis for twelve years. *Jazz Times* magazine wrote of Owen: "Paula Owen is the best-kept secret in vocal jazz."

Owen's recordings include "Red, Green and Blue" with vocalist Everett Greene, "What Is This Magic Happening?" with Ron Enyard, and "So Nice To Be With You" featuring saxophonist Ernie Krivda.

PHOTO CREDIT: LARRY GOSHEN

PAULA OWEN

Bill Penick

Bill Penick was born January 4, 1932 and was raised in Indianapolis, Indiana. He attended Crispus Attucks High School and studied saxophone for two years before joining the Hampton Family Band in the late '40s. He performed in the U.S. Army Military Band in the early '50s, and returned to Indianapolis for a successful music career. Penick performed with many jazz greats from the famed Indiana Avenue music scene. He was inducted into the Indianapolis Jazz Foundation Hall of Fame in 2009.

Carl Perkins

Pianist Carl Perkins was born in Indianapolis on August 16, 1928. Perkins toured with such artists as Big Jay McNeely and Tiny Bradshaw. In 1949, he moved to the West Coast. He played with the Oscar Moore Trio from 1953 to '54, and then performed with the Max Roach-Clifford Brown Quintet. In 1956, he played with bassist Curtis Counce. Perkins can be heard on recordings with such artists as Chet Baker, Jim Hall and Art Pepper. His final session was in 1958. It included his 24-bar tune "Grooveyard." This recording featured saxophonist Harold Land. Carl Perkins passes away on March 17, 1958.

Kenny Phelps

PHOTO CREDIT: LARRY GOSHEN

KENNY PHELPS

Kenny Phelps, drummer and CEO of the Owl Music Group, attended Crispus Attucks High School in Indianapolis, Indiana. In 1994 he performed in the Steve Allee release of "Magic Hour" and has since made many recordings, including one with singer Cynthia Layne. Kenny Phelps is host of the WICR *Owl Music Group Radio Show,* and toures nationally with Grammy Award-winning singer Dee Dee Bridgewater.

King Pleasure

Singer King Pleasure (Clarence Beeks) was born in Oakdale, Indiana, on March 24, 1922. He popularized the vocalese form of vocalizing jazz solos. In 1952, Pleasure won a talent competition at Harlem's Apollo, singing "Moody's Mood For Love." He recorded on the Prestige label and released several albums. King retired and moved to California. His recordings influenced such vocalese-lovers as Georgie Fame and the Manhattan Transfer. He died on March 21, 1981.

Clifford Ratliff

Clifford Ratliff was born on June 29, 1947 in Indianapolis. He began playing trumpet professionally on Indiana Avenue at the age of sixteen. After graduating from Crispus Attucks High School, Ratliff spent four years in the U.S. Air Force touring Southeast Asia with the USO. After returning to Indiana and receiving a music major at Indiana State University, he continued to perform with some of the top musicians in the Indianapolis area. In 1995, Clifford was a permanent member and recorded with the popular Small Talk Quintet. Ratliff became a prominent musician in the Indianapolis area. He performed regularly with the Jimmy Coe Big Band, and continues to play top jazz clubs around Indianapolis.

PHOTO CREDIT: LARRY GOSHEN

CLIFFORD RATTIFF

Melvin Rhyne

Pianist/organist Melvin Rhyne was born on October 12, 1936 in Indianapolis. His father, Aldrich Rhyne, was a ragtime pianist who provided Melvin the opportunity to grow up in a musical environment. Rhyne attended Crispus Attucks High School in 1949. In 1950, he performed with the R&B group The Monarchs. In 1956, Rhyne switched from piano to the organ. He later became more prominent on the Hammond B-3. Rhyne performed in local nightclubs such as the Turf Bar, the HubBub, 19th Hole, 440 Club, the Missile Room and Cotton Club. At those clubs, Rhyne performed with Leroy Vinnegar, Freddie Hubbard, Virgil Jones and drummer "Killer" Ray Appleton. In 1959, while playing with guitarist Wes Montgomery at the Indianapolis Missile Room, saxophonist Cannonball Adderley discovered the trio. They received their first recording contract with Riverside Records. They recorded four albums: *Wes Montgomery Trio* (1959), and *Boss Guitar, Guitar On The Go* and *Portrait Of Wes* in 1963. Melvin performed and appeared with many great artists such as B.B. King, Della Reese, The

PHOTO CREDIT: LARRY GOSHEN

MELVIN RHYNE

Four Tops, Roland Kirk, Jimmy Coe and many others. In 2008, Rhyne recorded with Rob Dixon, Fareed Hague and drummer Kenny Phelps and produced a CD titled *Reinvention* on the Owl Records label. Melvin Rhyne passed away on March 5, 2013 at the age of 76.

Larry Ridley

Born September 3, 1937, Larry Ridley is an American Jazz bassist and educator. After hometown collaborations with the likes of Wes Montgomery and Fredie Hubbard, Indiana-born Ridley moved to New York. It was there that he performed with such heavyweights as Sonny Rollins, Max Roach, Slide Hampton and many top name artists. In the '60s, he was regular bassist with Thelonious Monk. Larry Ridley remains active as an educator and performer.

PHOTO CREDIT: LARRY GOSHEN

CLAUDE SIFFERLEN

Claude Sifferlen

Indianapolis-born Sifferlen attended Scecina High School and Marian College. He performed with Duke Ellington, Woody Herman and locally with the Baron VonOhlen Quartet. In the 1980s, he started a 25-year collaboration with saxophonist-clarinetist Frank Glover. Claude Sifferlen died on March 18, 2010. His solo recording titled "Every Time We Say Goodbye" was released in 2013, three years after his death.

Leroy Vinnegar

Leroy Vinnegar was born in Indianapolis on July 13, 1928. He is one of the world's best-known jazz bassists. Vinnegar has performed with great jazz artists including Charlie Parker, Sonny Stitt, Stan Getz, Barney Kessel and drummer Shelly Manne. In the 1960s, he performed and recorded with Sonny Rollins, Gerald Wilson, the Jazz Crusaders and Kenny Dorham, just to name a few. Leroy Vinnegar died on August 3,1999 at the age of 71.

PHOTO CREDIT: DUNCAN SCHIEDT

Left to right: Benny Barth and Leroy Vinnegar

Steve Weakley

Indianapolis musician Steve Weakley picked up his first guitar at age eleven. As a Crispus Attucks High School graduate, he performed on famous Indiana Avenue with the R&B group The Girl Watchers. In the '70s he recorded several albums with Funk Inc., which included *Chicken Lickin'* and *Superfunk*. Members of Funk Inc. included Gene Barr, Cecil Hunt, Jimmy Munford, Bob Watley and Steve Weakley. One of their albums on the Prestige label reached the number 9 spot on the Billboard top 100. He later recorded with Billy Wooten on the highly collectable recording *In This World*. He continues to perform in the Indianapolis area.

PHOTO CREDIT: LARRY GOSHEN

STEVE WEAKLEY

Russell Webster

PHOTO CREDIT: LARRY GOSHEN

RUSSELL WEBSTER

Saxophonist Russell Webster, dubbed the "Whistling Postman," received classical training at Arthur Jordan Conservatory of Music and Crispus Attucks High School in Indianapolis. While underage, he received an early intro into jazz by performing in Indiana clubs with local greats Erroll Grandy and Leroy Vinnegar. Webster also performed with national entainers by sitting-in on the Avenue with musicians like Duke Ellington and Cab Calloway. After performing in the Army Band, he returned to Indiana and played saxophone with the Jimmy Coe Band, Reginald DuValle, Dave Young, J.J. Johnson, The Hamptons, the Montgomery Brothers and many others. Russell Webster died in September of 2007.

Pharez Whitted

PHOTO CREDIT: LARRY GOSHEN

PHAREZ WHITTED

Pharez Whitted, the son of late singer and bassist Virtue Hampton, was born into a family of twelve children that all played musical instruments. Pharez started trumpet at age nine and eventually earned a master's degree from Indiana University's Jacobs School of Music. He recorded his first album with Motown Records in 1994 and has been recording solo albums ever since. He performed at Carnegie Hall, a presidential inauguration, Billboard Music Awards and shared the stage with such distinguished performers as Bradford Maralis, George Duke, Elvin Jones, Nancy Wilson and many others.

Billy Wooten

Indiana-born Billy Wooten has been an international performer and recording artist for many years. His main instruments are the vibraharp and marimbas. He has performed for many dignitaries such as the President of Hungary, the Latin American Ambassador, the Prime Ministers of the Baltic States, and the President of the United States. He performed on television in such shows as *Party Time Royale* and *Blues with a Feeling*. Wooten hosted the WIFE Radio show *Jazz After Dark*. Billy has recorded for many national labels including Chess, Atlantic, United Artists and Blue Note. In addition to his own recordings, he has performed on major labels with Richard Evans & The Soulful Strings, and guitarist Grant Green. Billy Wooten passed away in March of 2016.

BILLY WOOTEN

David Young

Indianapolis resident David Young majored in music at Kentucky State College, Butler and Indiana University. After completing military service with the Third Armored Division Band, David performed in New York with the George Russell Sextet. They recorded *Jazz In The Space Age*, *The George Russell Sextet At The Five Spot*, *Statuspunk*, and *The George Russell Sextet In Kansas City*. He performed and toured with the Lionel Hampton Orchestra.

PHOTO CREDIT: DUNCAN SCHIEDT

Left to right: David Baker (trombone), David Young (sax), Larry Ridley (bass) annd Wes Montgomery (guitar) (1958)

While with Hampton, he recorded the jazz album *The Newport Uproar*. David has performed and recorded with many other major artists such as Frank Foster, Jack McDuff and The Grover Mitchell Jazz Orchestra. He recorded his own album, the self-titled *David Young*, on the Mainstream label. David toured with the Duke Ellington Orchestra under the direction of Mercer Ellington. He has accompanied such artists as Sarah Vaughn, Ella Fitzgerald, Joe Williams, Nancy Wilson, Tony Bennett, Della Reese, and the great Cab Calloway. Saxophonist David Young died in Feburary of 2009.

Left to right: Michel Brown and Chatterbox proprietor David Andrichik (On stage at the Chatterbox, 1996)

Jazz Notables

Al Cobine

Al Kiger

Alan Reeve

Amy Stephens

Aretta La Marre

Barry Kettery

Bill Lancton

Bill Moss

Bill Myers

Carl Hines

Caroll De Camp

Cathy Morris

Charlie Smith

Chris Pyle

Chuck Carter

Claude Sifferlen

Claude Thornhill

Dan Smith

Dave Atkins

Dick Laswell

Dick Reeves

Don Wilhite

Donna Lively Clark

Earl Coe

Evan Drybread

Everett Greene

Frank Smith

Frank Steans

Fred Monroe

Fred Withrow

Gary Walters

Gene Markiewicz

George Mack

Gregg Bacon

Hal Smith

Hans Sturm

Harold Cardwell

Harold Gooch

Jack Helsley

Jack Phelan

James Bell

James Spaulding

Jan Aldridge Clark

Janiece Jaffe

Jeff Deherdt

Jerry Coker

Jim Albrecht

Jim Edison

Jim Farrelly

Jimmy Munford

Joe Deal

John Hill

John Huber

John Spicknall

John Von Ohlen

Jonathan Wood

Jozell Carter

Julie Spencer

Ken Gotschall

Keni Washington

Kenny Kipp

Kenny Phelps

Kevin Anker

Kevin Johnson

Music on the Rise

There are many new and exciting entertainers performing in the Indiana area. Here are just a few we feel should be recognized. Remember, you do not need to be a true Indiana native to be considered a Hoosier, just live here long enough to leave your roots.

Charlie Ballantine

Indianapolis-based gritarist Charlie Ballantine is well-known for headlining jazz events such as the Penrod Art Festival and the Indianapolis Jazz Fest. He performs at the popular Jazz Kitchen and Chatterbox Jazz Club, and tours nationally in places like Chicago and Detroit. As a recording artist, he has released six albums, *Green* (2015), *Providence* (2016), *Where is My Mind* (2017), the music of Bob Dylan, *Life is Brief* in 2018, *Vonnegut* (2020) and *Cold Coffee* (2021).

PHOTO CREDIT: LARRY GOSHEN

CHARLIE BALLANTINE

Jenn Cristy

A native of Tennessee now living in Indiana, Jenn Cristy began playing piano at an early age. While attending college at Indiana University, she was hired by John Mellencamp as a background vocalist for his 2001 album and tour of *Cuttin' Heads*. As a popular keyboardist/singer she continues to headline and perform both in Indiana and nationally.

PHOTO CREDIT: LARRY GOSHEN

JENN CRISTY

Sophie Faught

A Native of Indianapolis, Sophie studied both classical piano and alto/tenor saxophone. She performed with the University of Indianapolis' big band and has won several outstanding soloist awards. She performes jazz as a sideman and with her own group at the Chatterbox, Jazz Kitchen and other points across the Midwest.

PHOTO CREDIT: MARK SHELDON

SOPHIE FAUGHT

Amanda Gardier

Based out of Indianapolis, Amanda Gardier performs saxophone as a band-leader, session musician and sideman. She sometimes performs and tours with guitarist Charlie Ballantine and is featured on several of his recordings. A recording release of her own, titled *Empathy* (August 2018) and *Flyover Country (2020)*. She continues to tour around the Indiana area. She is now married to guitarist Charlie Ballantine and has a daughter named River.

PHOTO CREDIT: LARRY GOSHEN

AMANDA GARDIER

Sarah Grain

Indianapolis born Sarah Grain attended North Central High School and studied at Indiana University. She sings and performs on guitar with her own band, Sara Grain & the Billions of Stars. Their album, *Something Wild,* was released in 2017.

PHOTO CREDIT: LARRY GOSHEN

SARAH GRAIN

Mina Keohane

Mina Keohane, composer, instrumentalist and vocalist, was born in Fort Walton Beach, Florida, and now lives in Indianapolis. She studied composition and voice at Berklee College of Music. She performs with her own group, Mina & the Flying Machine, and plays keyboard for Sara Grain and the Billions of Stars.

PHOTO CREDIT: LARRY GOSHEN

MINA KEOHANE

Gwynneth Reitz

PHOTO CREDIT: LARRY GOSHEN

GWYNNETH (BURGINS) REITZ

Evansville native Gwynneth Reitz started her music career performing with the electronica duo Lunar Event. With Gwynneth on keyboard and Derek Osgood on guitar/vocals, they created a sound between underground, mainstream and pop. They later added Jon Harmon on bass and Drew Reed on drums. They recorded one album in 2002 titled *This Transparency.* Gwynneth was lead singer of the four-piece band There Are Ghosts. This band produced their own original material and consists of Tony Reitz on guitar, Jon Harmon, guitar, Andrew Mahoney, bass and Mike Theodore on drums.

Freeze Frame

(MISCELLANEOUS PHOTOGRAPHS)

PURE GOLD

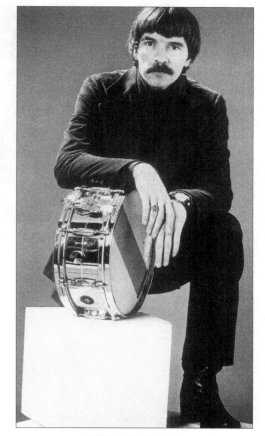

RON ENYARD

THE HAMILTON MOVEMENT

LIGHT 3D

DAVE MORGAN TRIO

AL WALTON TRIO WITH JOY SMITH

TOGETHERNESS IS

WE-3

YOUNG SET

THE KELLY JAY ORCHESTRA

JERRY DICKERSON

PHOTO CREDIT: LARRY GOSHEN

GERARDO BECERRA

PURE FUNK

CHERYL ASH-SIMPSON

BILLY BALL
& THE UPSETTERS

STEVE MASON TRIO

WITNESS

PHOTO CREDIT: LARRY GOSHEN

JARED MICHAEL

WORDS OF WISDOM

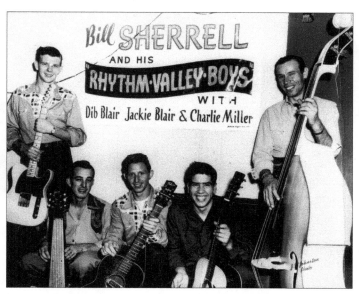

BILL SHERRELL AND HIS RHYTHM VALLEY BOYS

Photograph Credits

Art Adams, Art Adams collection

Amos Arthur, Arthur's Music Store

"Bouncin' Bill" Baker, Bill Baker collection

Boyd Bennett, Boyd Bennett collection

The Blue Angels, Lillian Boles

The Boppers, Jimmy Guilford

Jimmy Clendening, Don Holt

Jimmy Coe Orchestra, Jimmy Coe

The Contemporaries, Gerald Ruark

The Counts, Dave Williams

The Crowns, L. Goshen

The Deb Tones, Jimmy Mack

Danny Dollar, Morgan Schumacher collection

DownBeats, Morgan Schumacher collection

Chuck Berry & Morgan Schumacher, L. Goshen

Jackie De Shannon, L. Goshen

The Fascinators, Don Kelley

The Five Stars, Jim Bruhn

The Four Freshmen, Duncan Schiedt

The Four Sounds, Jimmy Guilford

Jimmy Ganzberg & Jimmy Mack, L. Goshen

Jimmy Ganzberg, J. Ganzberg

1958 Jimmy Coe Group, Jerry Williams collection

Larry Gardner, L. Gardner

Gary Gillespie, Don Kelley collection

Hampton Sisters, Virtue Hampton

Duke Hampton Band, Virtue Hampton

Ronnie Haig, L. Goshen

Bobby Helms, Jerry Williams collection

Johnny & The Pyramids, Dan Beach

Keetie & The Kats, Don Holt & Loughery's Studio

Larry Lee & Keith Phillips, L. Gardner

The Labels, Don Kelley

Bobby Lewis, Bobby Lewis collection

Jimmy Mack, J. Mack collection

Lonnie Mack, L. Mack

Jack Morrow, Loughery's Studio

Nooney Rickett, Don Kelley

Rooker & The Rockers, Don Holt

Jerry Seifert, Don Kelley

The Showmen, Doug Sterns

The Crowns Live, L. Goshen

Larry Goshen, Herb Goshen

Jerry Lee Williams & The Crowns, L. Goshen

Tommy Wills, Tommy Wills

Dale Wright, D. Wright & Dr. Pepper

Al Young, Al Young

Jimi Hendrix & Al Young, Al Young

Boys Next Door, Don Holt

The Checkmates Ltd., Sonny Charles

The Chosen Few, Carl Storie

Coven, Steve Ross

The Dawn Five, Don Holt

The Heavy, Phil Thompson

The Highlighters, Jason Yoder

The Idle Few, Ron Benneth

Jackson 5, Don Kelley collection

Joys Of Life, Jim Albrecht

The Knightsmen, Karl Hinkle

The McCoys, Bob Berry

Keith Murphy & Daze, Keith Murphy

Reb Porter, Jimmy Mack

The Rivieras, Miriam Linna

The Sentimentals, B&L Photographers

The Shy Ones, Bonnie McDowell

Sounds Unlimited, Wayne Wilson

The Torkays, Keith Murphy

The Accents, Vince Sanders

Andy Anderson & The Jets, J. Ganzberg

Marden Baker Quartet, L. Goshen

The Blue Tones, Cale & Whyte

By/Counts, M. James

The Cavaliers, L. Goshen

Ray Churchman, Louis J. McMahon & Melvin James collection

The Classmen, M. James

The Crackerjacks, L. Goshen

Bobby Dark & Darlene Dowler, D. Dowler

The Dawnbeats #2, L. Gardner

Del & The Road Runners, D. Bailey

Bill Stewart, Delbert Bailey & Charlie Rich, D. Bailey

The Pacesetters, D. Demaree

Danny Dollar & The Coins, L. Goshen

The Dukes, Jim Hickman

The Epics, P. Hutchinson —The Epics, Art Adams

The Five Checks, Cale & Whyte

The Five Chords, D. Kelley

The First Impression, Louis J. McMahon & Melvin James collection

Flo Garvin, F. Garvin

Suzanne Prince Band, Gilbert Gordon

Jimmy Guilford, J. Guilford

The Inner Circle, Guy Tarrents

Jess & The Jokers, J. Colburn

The Jewels, G. LeMaster

Sons Of The Pioneers, G. LeMaster

Jimmy & The Exceptions, G. Tarrents

Orly Knutson Trio, J. Ganzberg

Tommy Lam, Jerry Williams collection

Jimmy McDaniels & Pete Funk, L. Goshen

The Monograms, Bob Bernard

Index

MTV, 155, 158
Mulligan, Gerry, 164, 218
Mullinix, Tom, 234
Mullins, D. C., 195
Mumbles Blues, 30
Munford, Jimmy, 221, 241, 245
Muncie, 158, 173, 237
Murphy, Keith, 60, 66, 259
Murphy, Wally, 47
Music Stand Records, 121
Must Believe In Magic, 200
MX 80, 126
My Boy Flat Top, 6
My Dear My Darling, 10
My Heart, 35, 125
My Lai Massacre, 108
My Love Just Ain't Getting Through,
34
My Paradise, 18
My Special Angel, 25
My Special Love, 148
My Sweet Cindy, 22
My Sweet Lord, 108
My Weakness, 113
Myers, Bill, 170, 234, 245
Myers, Shadow, 117
Myers, Toby, 123, 125, 133
Myriad, 235
Myron Murry, 74, 82
Mystical Adventures, 225
Myths For A New Millennium, 181

N

Nabor Records, 93
Name Your Adventure, 215
Naptown Strutters, 234
Naptown, 62, 158
Nardini, Linda, 142
Narell, Andy, 144
Nashville, i, 4, 6, 41, 92, 118, 196-199,
206, 208
Nasser, Tony, 80
Nathan, Sid, 60
National College Jazz Competition,
222
National Endowment for the Arts Jazz
Performance award, 223
Naughty Child, 128
Nauseating Butterfly Records, 64
NBC, 32, 195, 215
ND Witnesses, 31

Neal, Kenny, 139
Neat, Dick, 92
Nebraska, 30
Needmore, Indiana, xi
Neilsen, Chris, 51
Nelson Jr., Oliver, 178, 227, 235
Nelson Sr., Oliver, 235
Nelson, Tracey, 118
Nelson, Willie, 25, 183
Nephew, Steve, 50
Ness, John, 82
Never Baby Never, 34
New Albany, 29
New Jazz Arranger of the Year award,
231
New York Blues Hall of Fame, 139
New York City, i, 2, 139, 226
New York Pops, 172
Newbold, Steve, 120, 132, 148
Newcomer, Carrie, 137, 152
Newman, David "Fathead", 220
Newman, Paul, 108
Newton, Wayne, 77
Next Bus South, 73
Nicholas Brothers, 16, 101
Nichols, Butch, 35
Nichols, Red, 222
Nichols, Steve, 124
Nick & Jerrys, 71
Nicoloff, Greg, 51
Nicoloff, Mike, 51
Niemiec, Ted, 117
Nightshade, Billy, 117
19th Hole, 239
Niverson, Richie, 66
Nixon, Richard M., 108
No Body Loves Me, 88
No Guarantees, 184
No Man's Land, 206
No Rain, 178
No Regrets, 173, 182
Noblesville, 183, 209
Noe, Timothy, 140
Noel, Jack, 198
Nolan, Larry "Big Twist", 139
North Central High School, 110, 169,
251
North Vernon, Indiana, 32
North, Jerry, 234
North, Tim, 141
Norton, Cathi, 191
Not The Spirit Of India, 64

Note Records, 34
November Rain, 165
Now Is Here, 62
Noworthy Records, 215
Nox, 149
Nugent, Ted, 125, 187
Nuss, Otto, 61
Nuvo Weekly Magazine, 186, 226

O

O'Banion, John, 153
O'Brook, Howard, 41
O'Connel, Helen, 230
O'Connor, Keith, 60, 66
Oakdale, 238
Oakley, Annie, 30
Obama, Barak, 226
Oddi, Jacklyn, 140
Officer, Al, 9, 84
Officer, Emmanuel, 140
Ogolini, Terry, 139
Oh How I Need You, 138
Oh The Girls, 125
Ohio, 19, 23, 31, 40, 91, 170, 179, 202,
237
Old Friends, New Friends, 222
Oldies Concerts, 141
Olive Lucy, 182
Oliver Syndrome, 191
Oliver, Kelly, 143, 175
Oliver, Sam, 88
Omega, 124
Omni, 198
On The Outside Looking In, 87
Once A Day, 207
One Flew Over the Cuckoo's Nest, 11,
44
One Last Chance, 64
One Tin Soldier, 51
One Track Mind, 139
Open Mind, 225
Orbison, Roy, 38, 44
Ordinary People, 136
Organ, Michael, 158
Oriental Hotel, 226
Orleans, Indiana, 187
Orly Knutson Trio, 92, 259
Ornung, Danny, 74, 82
Osborne, Bud, 6
Osborne, Greg "Oz", 51
Osborne, Greg, 55

About the Author

*B*esides being a respected musical historian, Larry Goshen is an accomplished musician and drummer who has performed with such groups as The Crowns, The Five Checks, and Sweetwater. Larry operates Face the Music, a photographic company specalizing in publicity photographs for celebrities. He lives in Historic Fountain Square in Indianapolis, Indiana.

CPSIA information can be obtained
at www.ICGtesting.com
Printed in the USA
LVHW061826200222
711572LV00008B/197

9 781955 622820